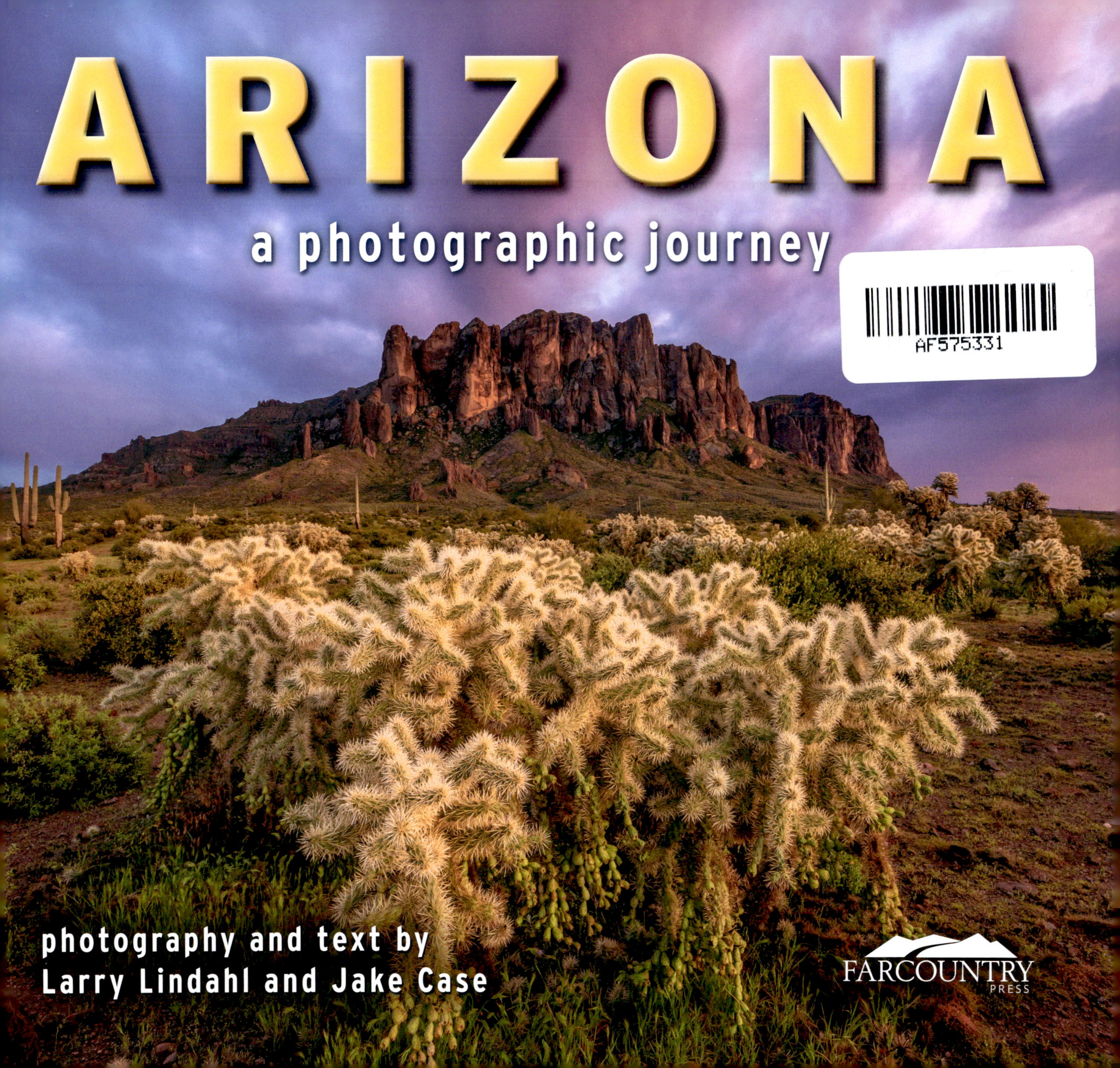
ARIZONA
a photographic journey
AF575331
photography and text by
Larry Lindahl and Jake Case
FARCOUNTRY
PRESS

To my love, Jane, who brings her sunshine and magic to my world every day.
— Larry Lindahl

To my wife Melissa, daughter Lennon, and parents Bill and Ruth who have always supported me. —Jake Case

Right: A prickly pear cactus displays a trio of vibrant flowers, with many more on the way. JAKE CASE

Far right: The Lower Salt River mirrors day's end at the rugged Bulldog Cliffs east of Phoenix. JAKE CASE

Title page: The crags of the Superstition Mountains tower over a stand of chain fruit cholla at Lost Dutchman State Park. JAKE CASE

Front cover: The Mazatzal Mountains catch a crimson sunset glow during a calm April evening at Bartlett Lake. The hills above the reservoir often come alive with wildflowers in the springtime. JAKE CASE

Back cover: A horse and rider pose on John Ford Point in Monument Valley Tribal Park. The popular vista honors the legendary movie director who, in 1939, filmed *Stagecoach,* the first movie made in the valley. LARRY LINDAHL

Following pages: A rainbow arcs into the White Pocket area of Vermilion Cliffs National Monument just south of the Utah border. LARRY LINDAHL

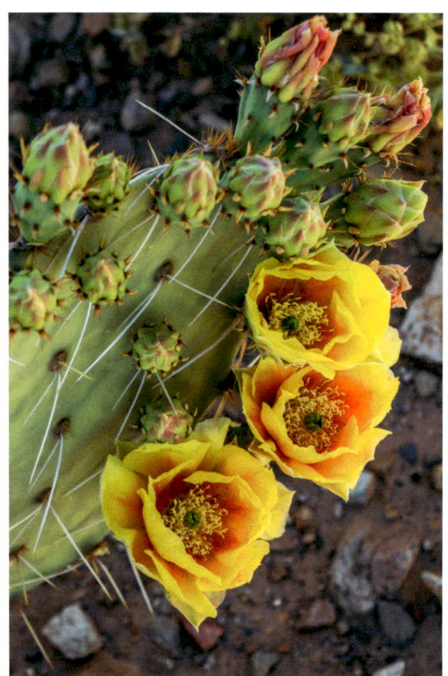

ISBN: 978-1-56037-842-6

Text by Larry Lindahl and Jake Case

Design by Steph Lehmann

For more information about our books, write Farcountry Press, P.O. Box 5630, Helena, MT 59604; call (800) 821-3874; or visit www.farcountrypress.com.

Produced in the United States of America. Printed in China.

28 27 26 25 24 1 2 3 4 5

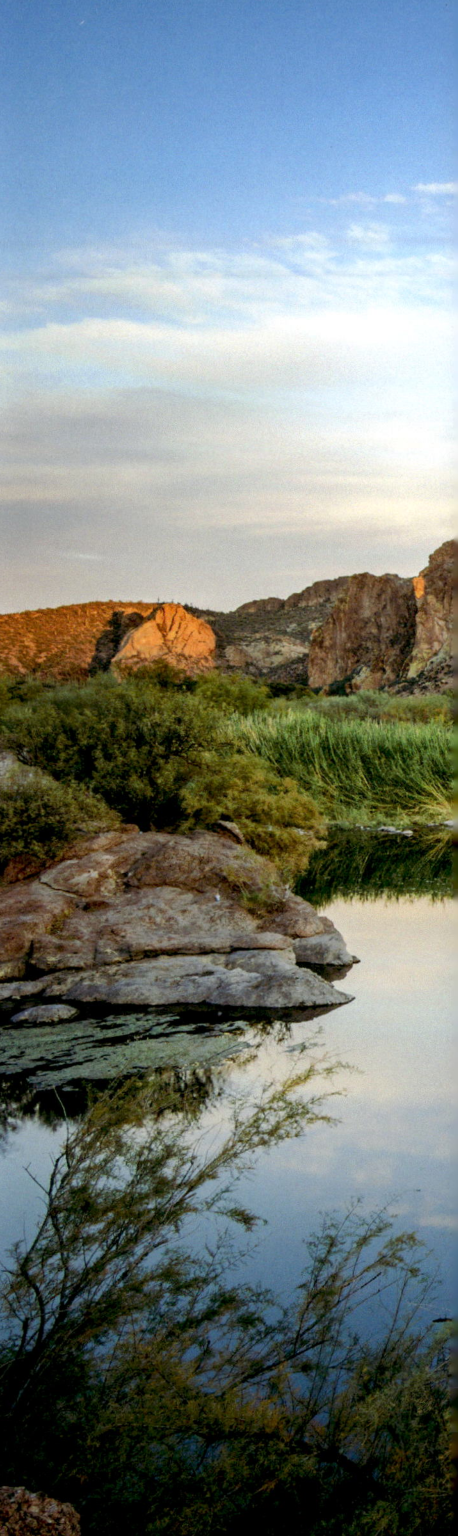

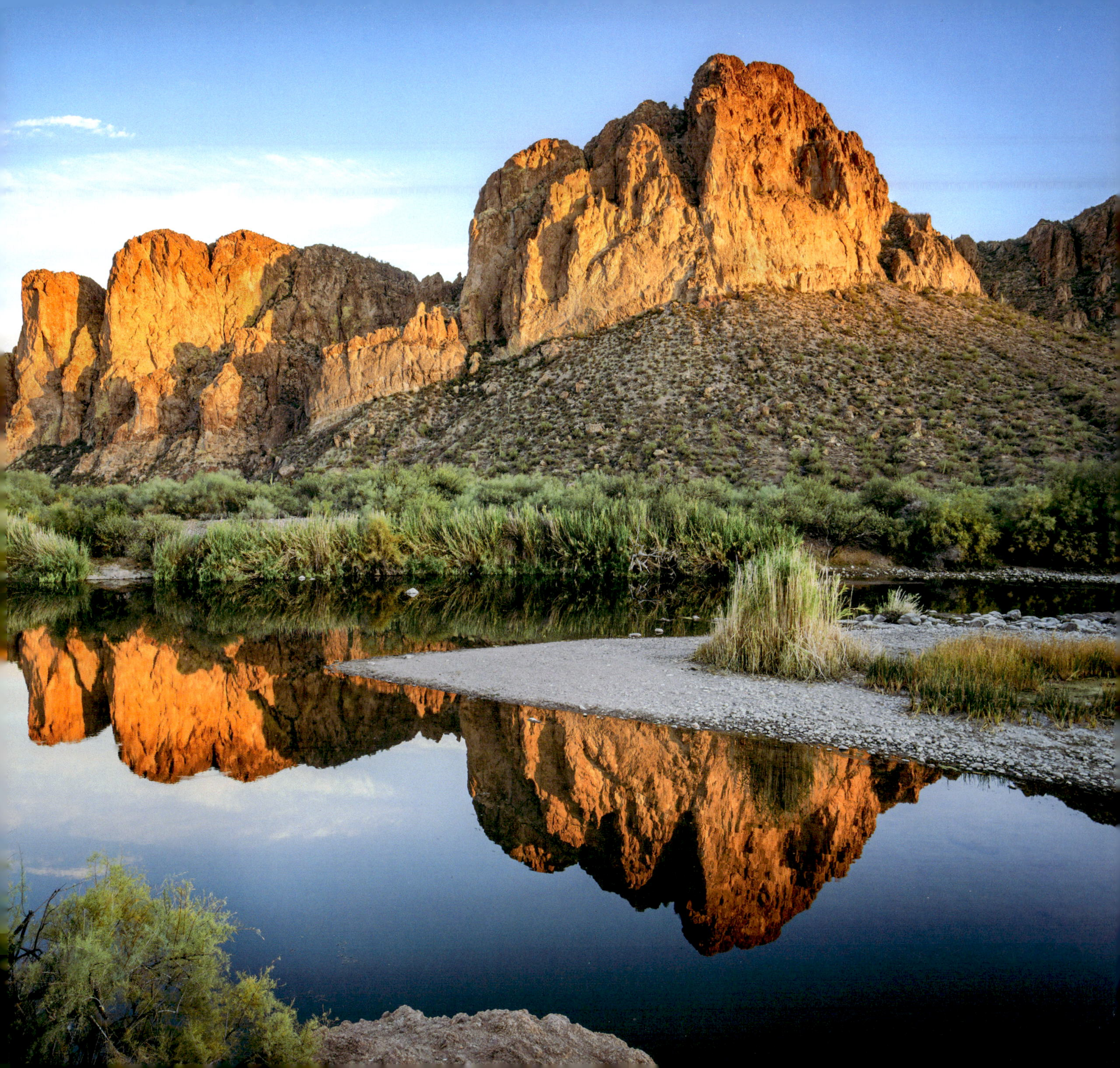

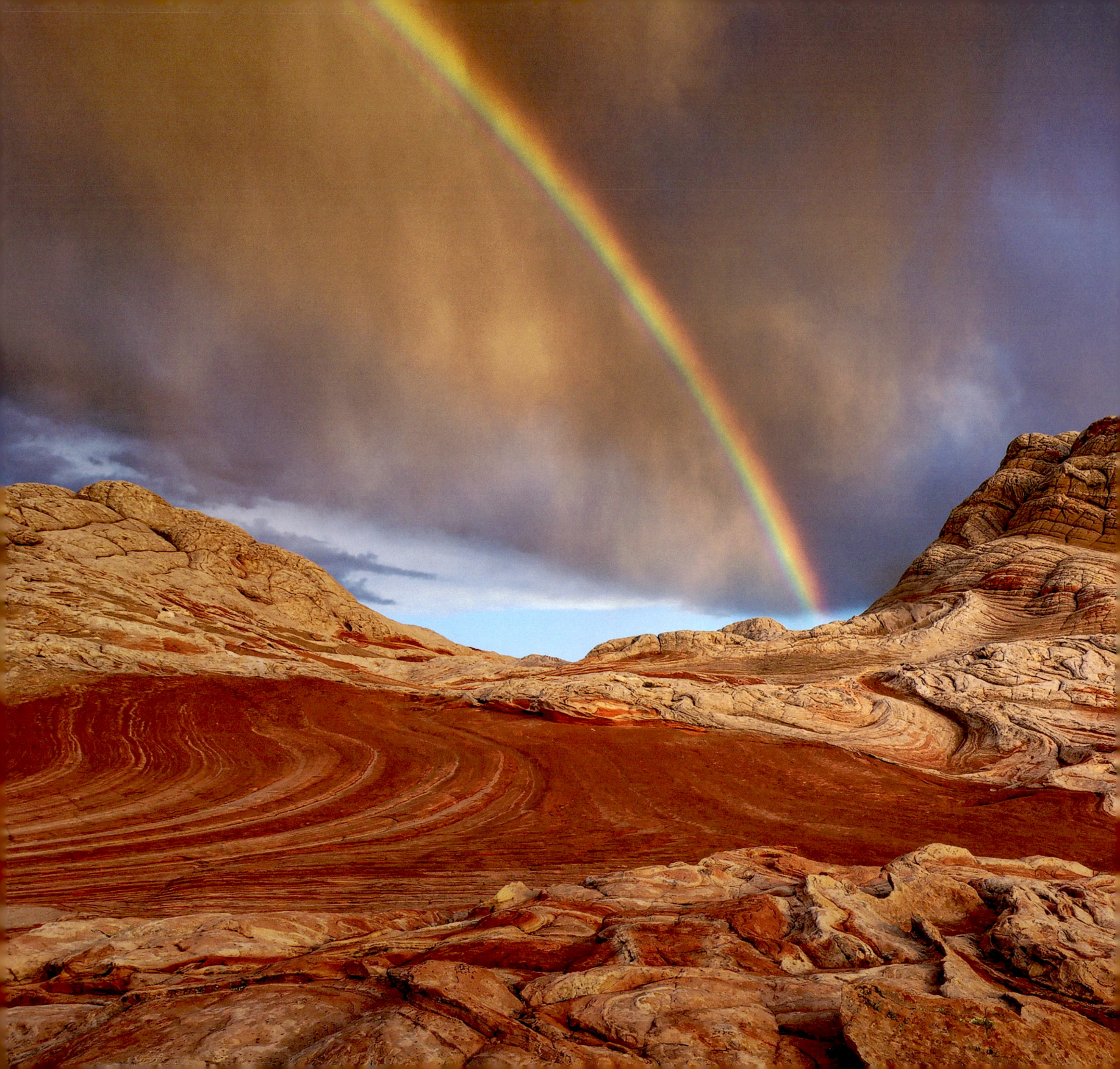

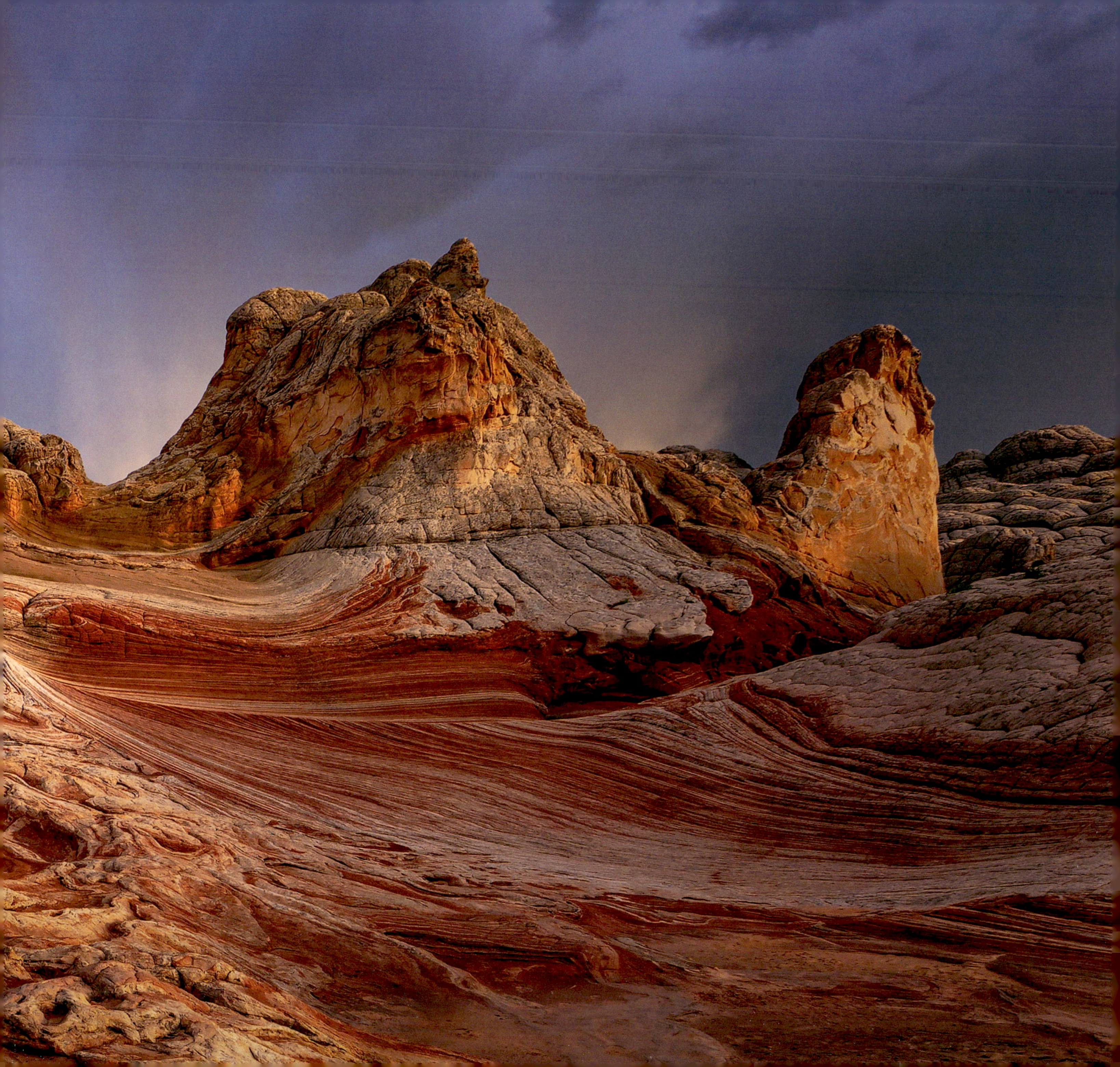

Right: A placid pool reflects lush greenery in West Fork Canyon, north of Sedona, in the Coconino National Forest. LARRY LINDAHL

Below: From the 7,000-foot Mogollon Rim, Horton Creek tumbles over sandstone and limestone in Tonto National Forest near Payson. LARRY LINDAHL

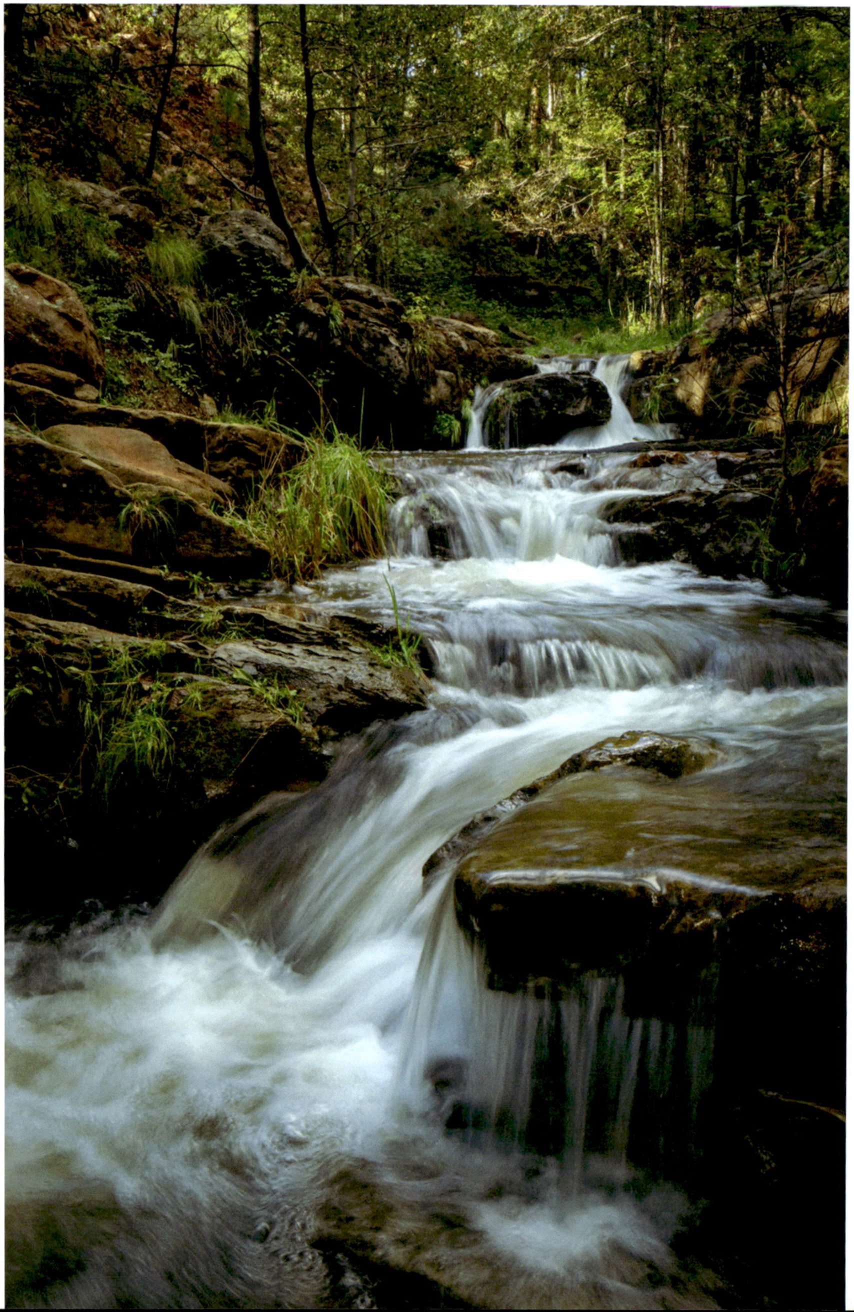

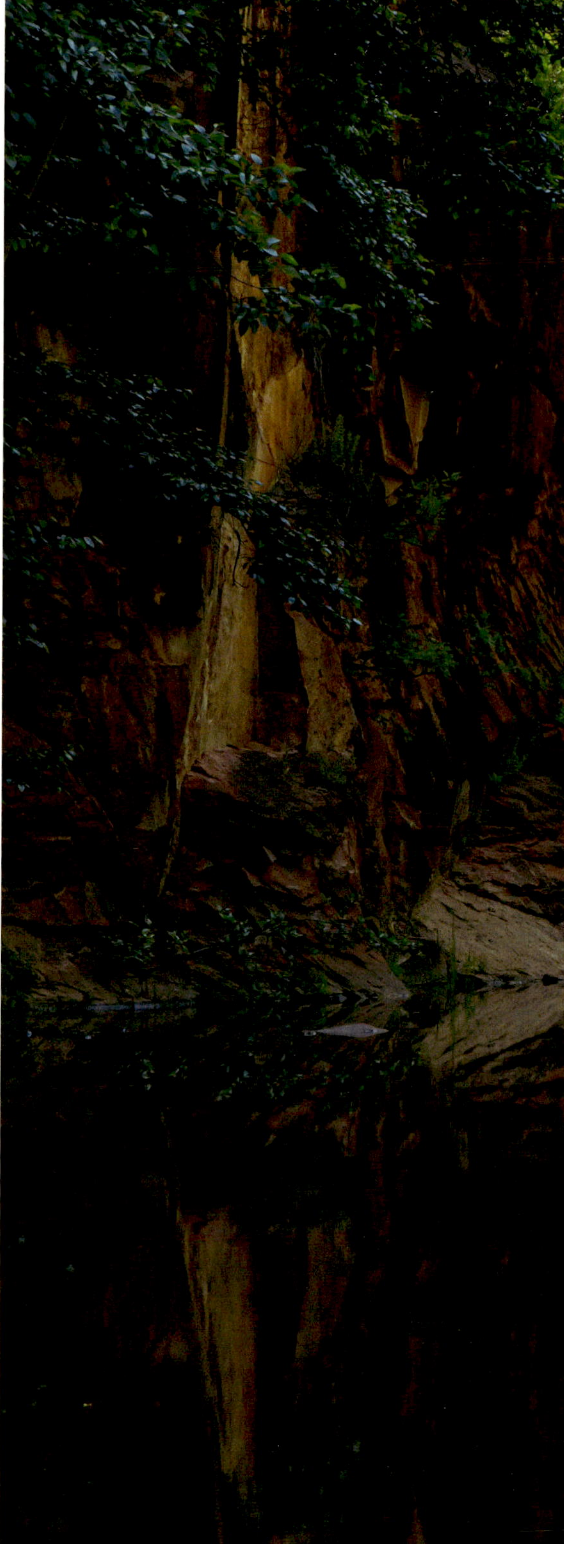

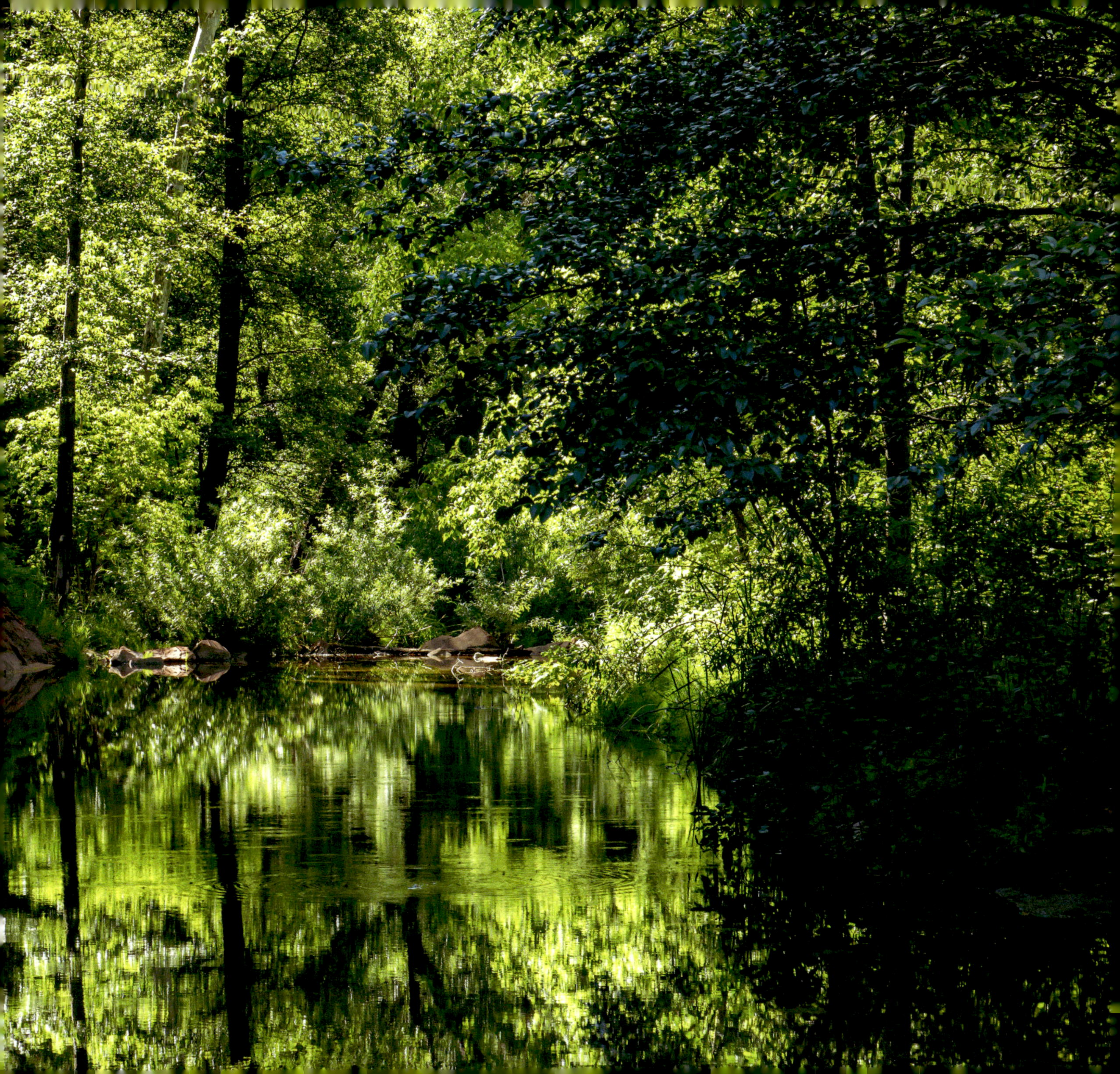

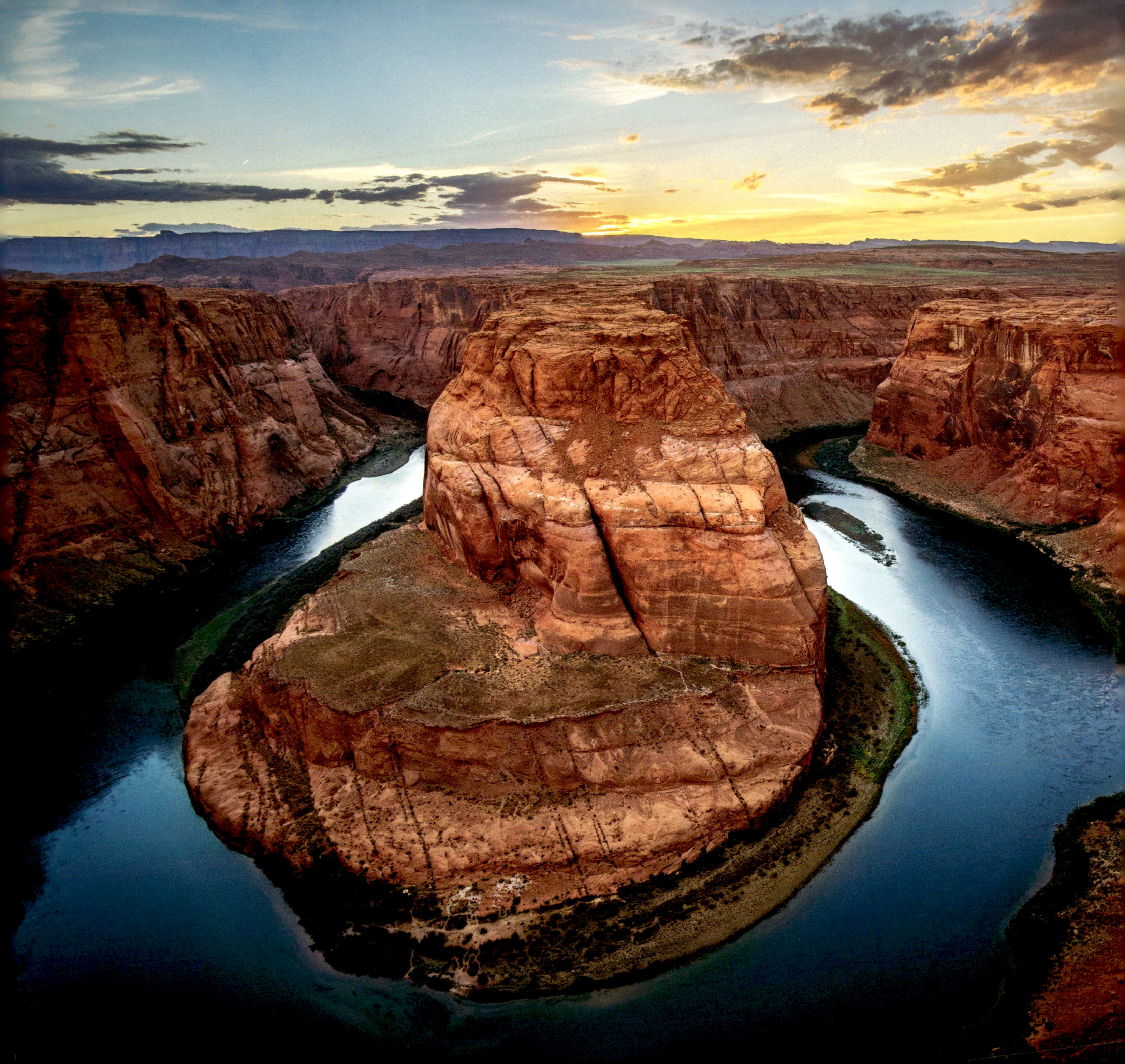

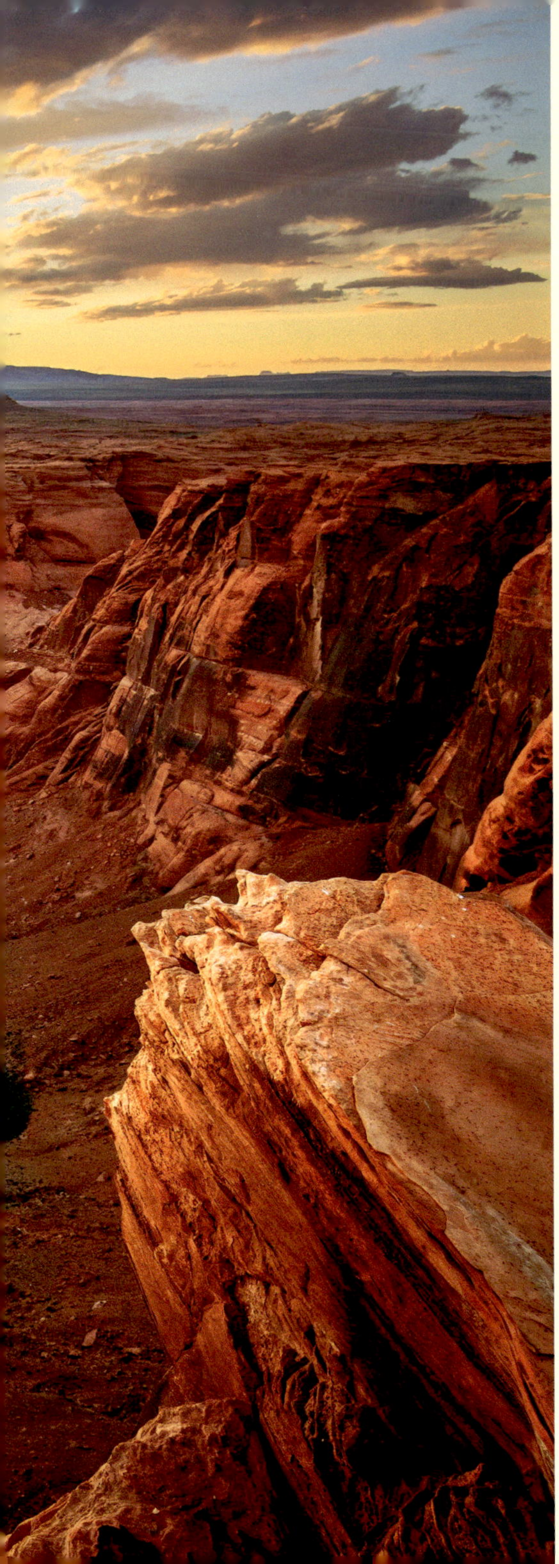

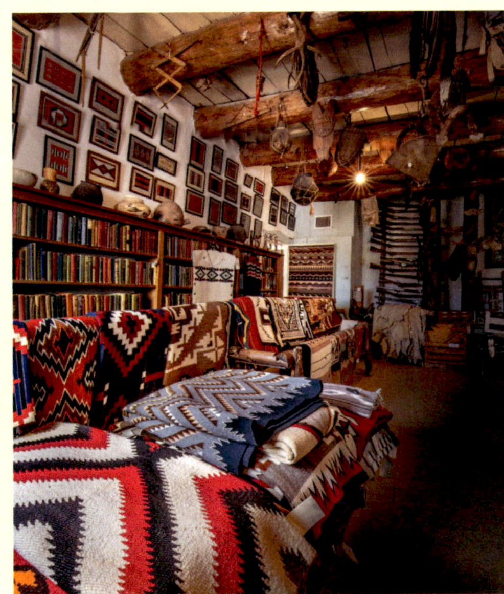

Left and below: Hubbell Trading Post, founded in 1878, is the oldest trading post on the Navajo Reservation still in operation. LARRY LINDAHL

Far left: The Colorado River makes a sharp 270-degree turn as it meanders through the 1,000-foot cliffs of Glen Canyon at Horseshoe Bend. JAKE CASE

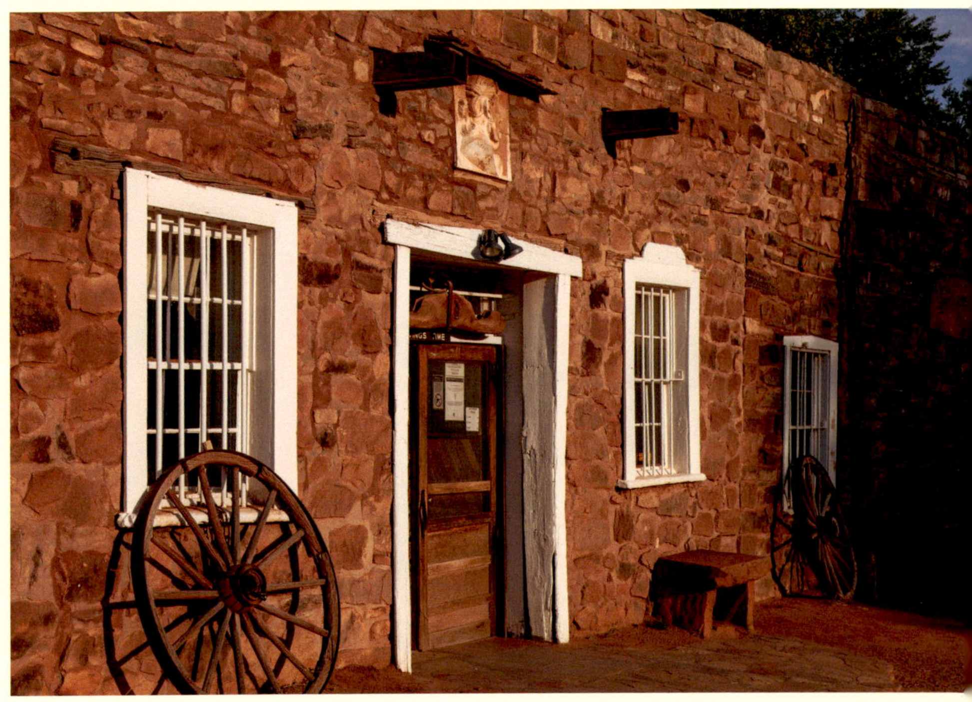

Right: A Native American pow wow dancer proudly wears a hand-beaded, deerskin shawl. LARRY LINDAHL

Far right: The San Francisco Peaks north of Flagstaff are remnants of an extinct stratovolcano, sacred land to the Navajo, Hopi, Havasupai, Zuni, Apache, and many other tribes of the region. LARRY LINDAHL

Below: Jerome, a "ghost town" of less than 500 residents, was once one of the richest copper mines in the Southwest. The funky town now hosts galleries, restaurants, historic hotels, and museums. LARRY LINDAHL

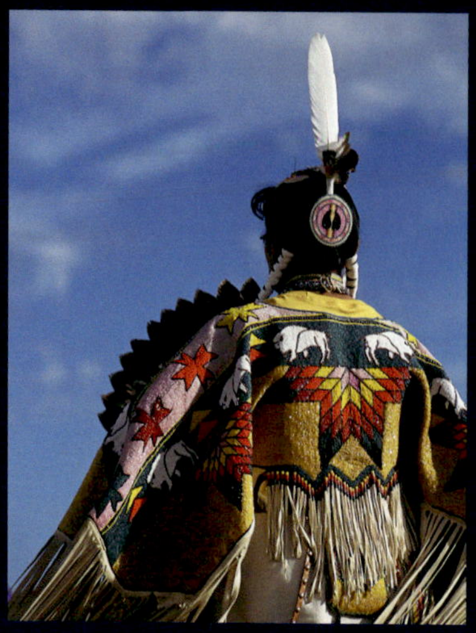

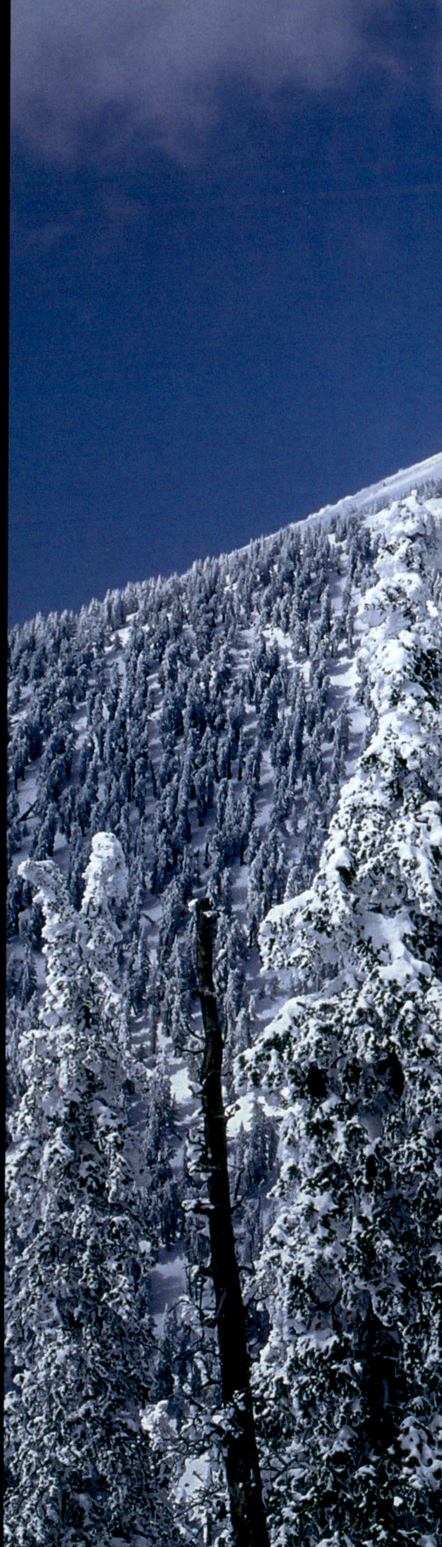

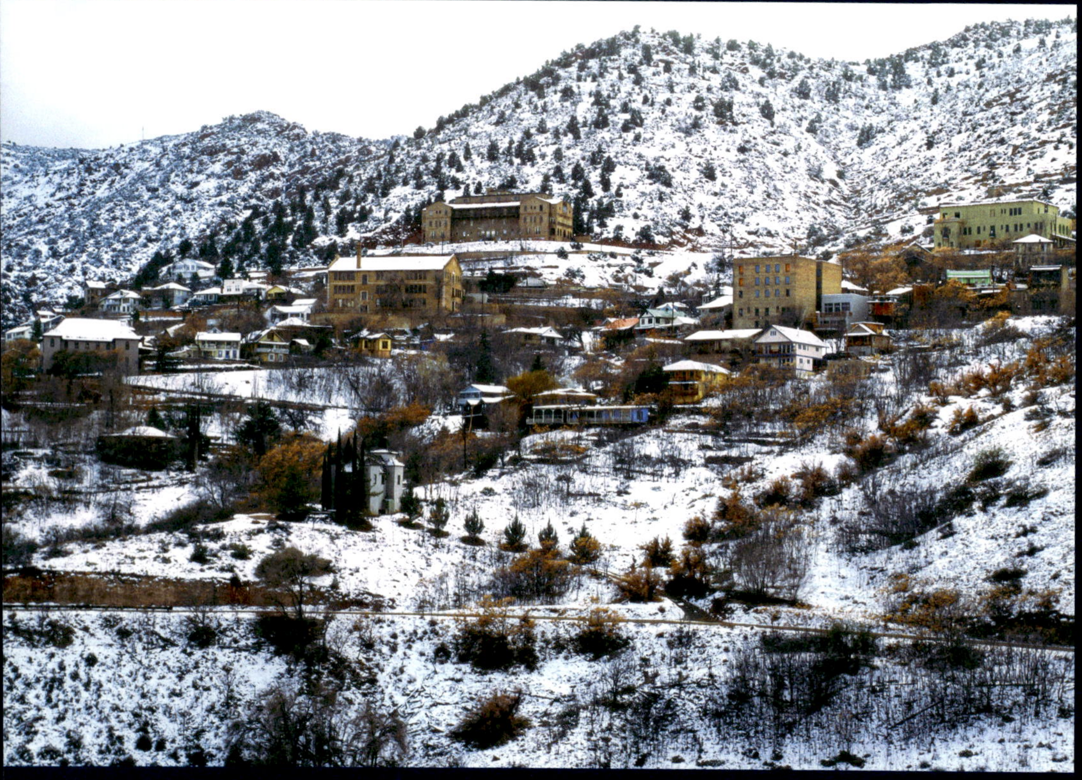

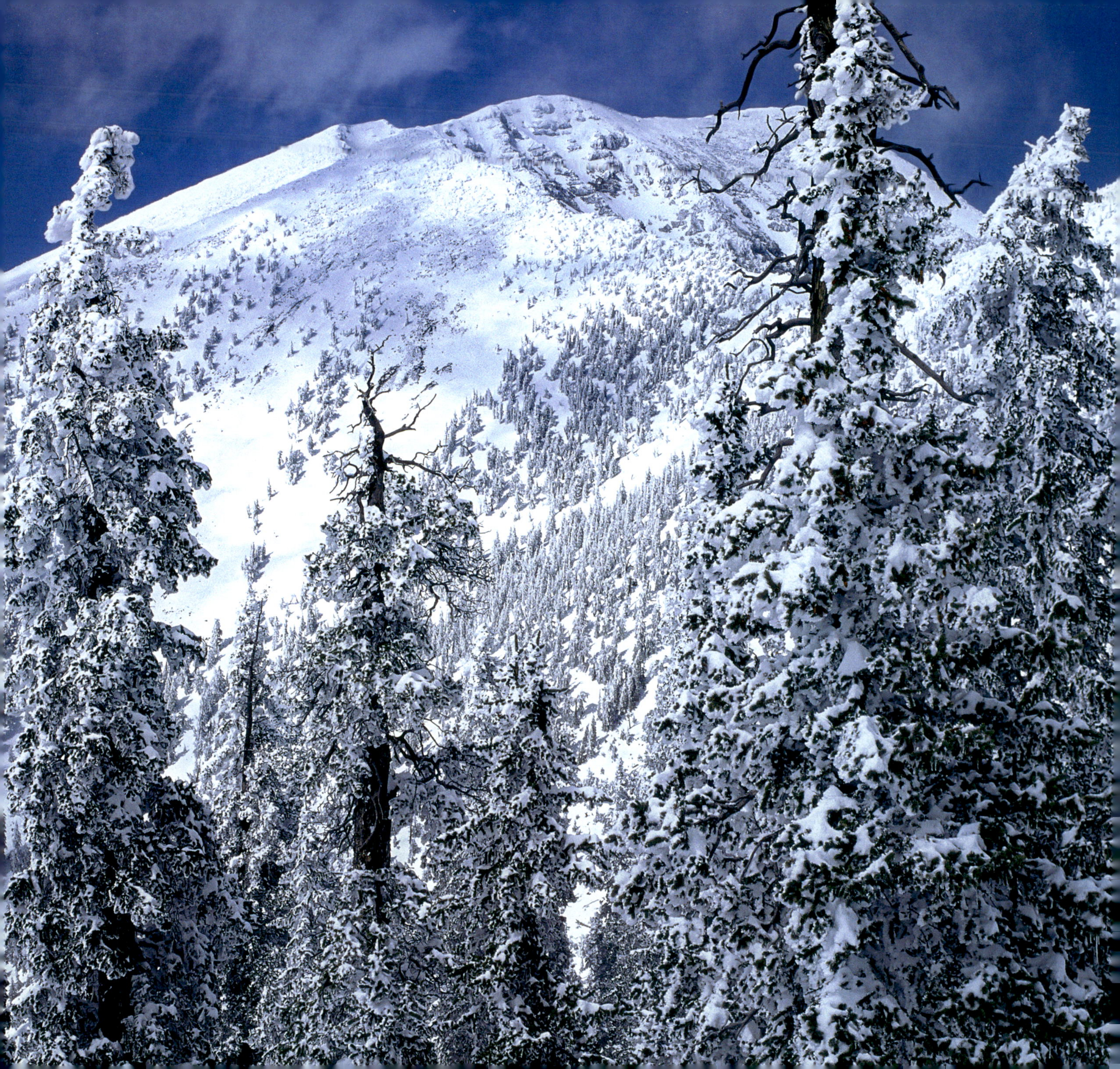

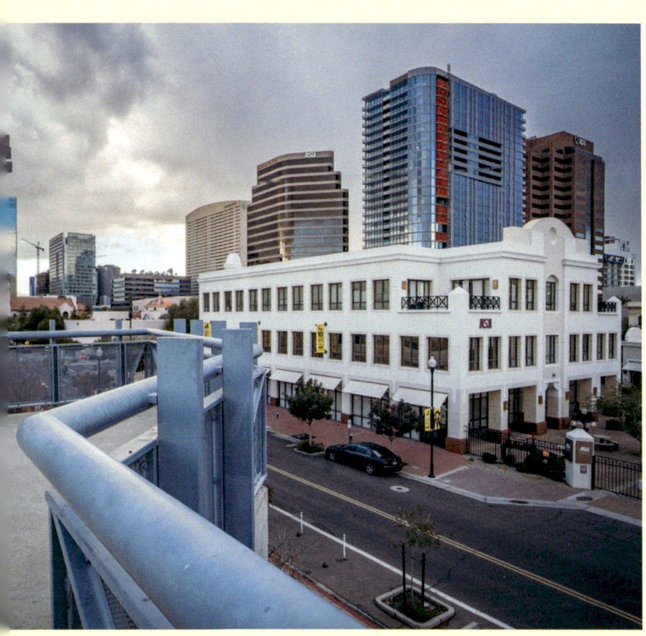

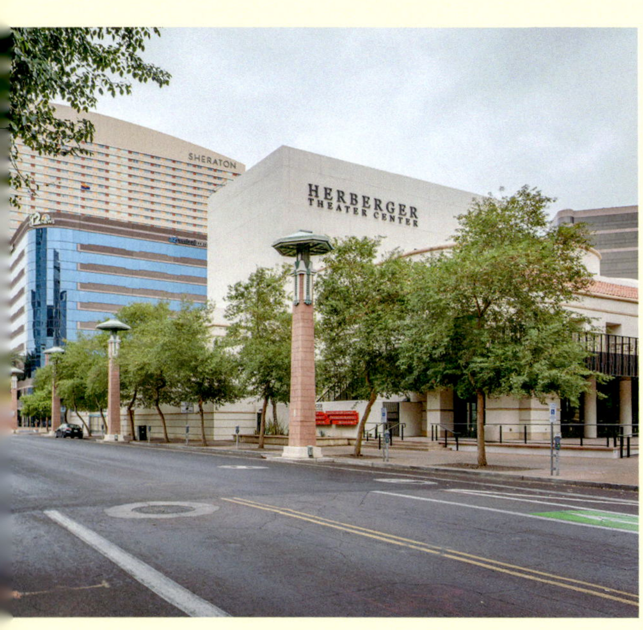
SHERATON
HERBERGER
THEATER CENTER

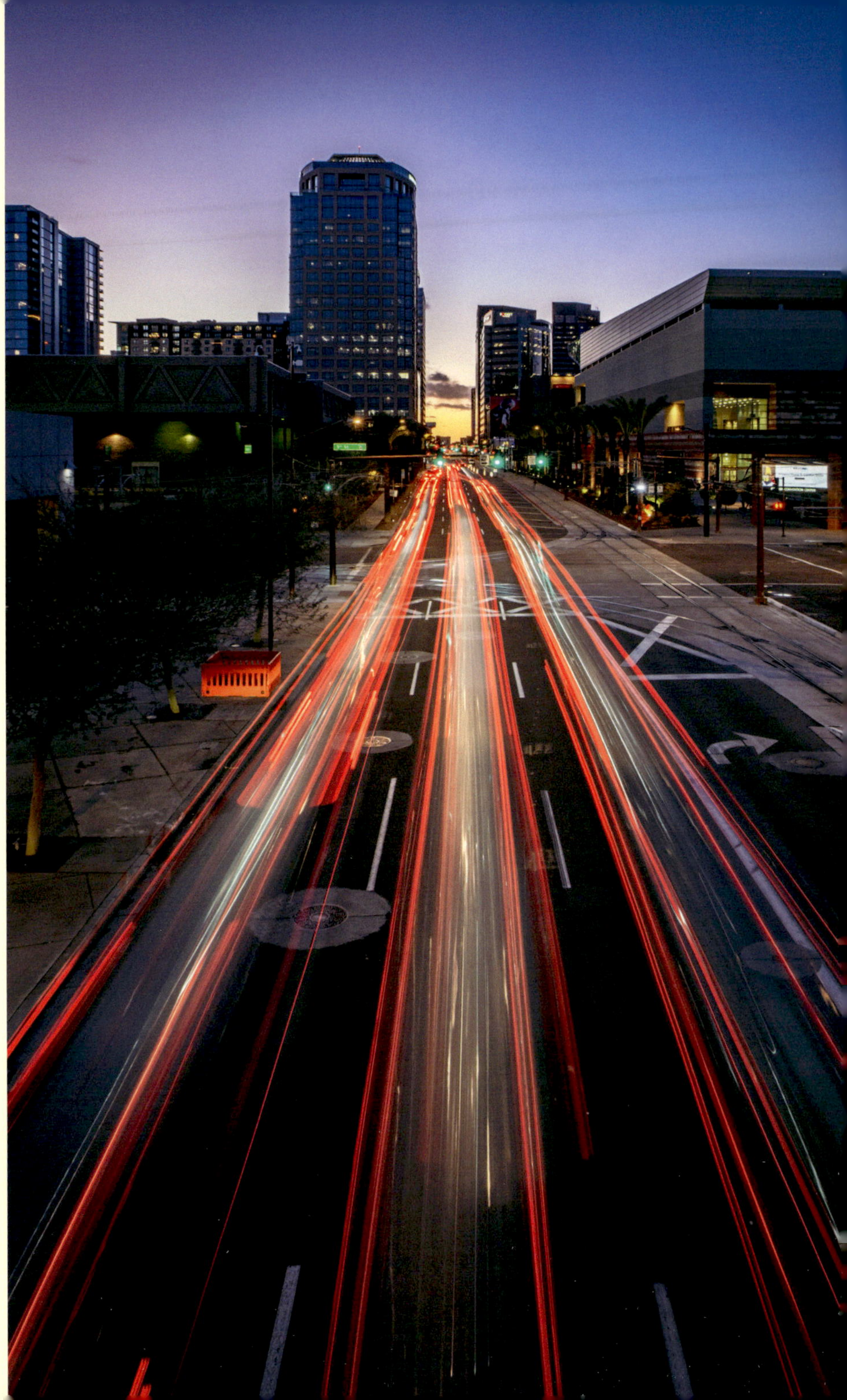

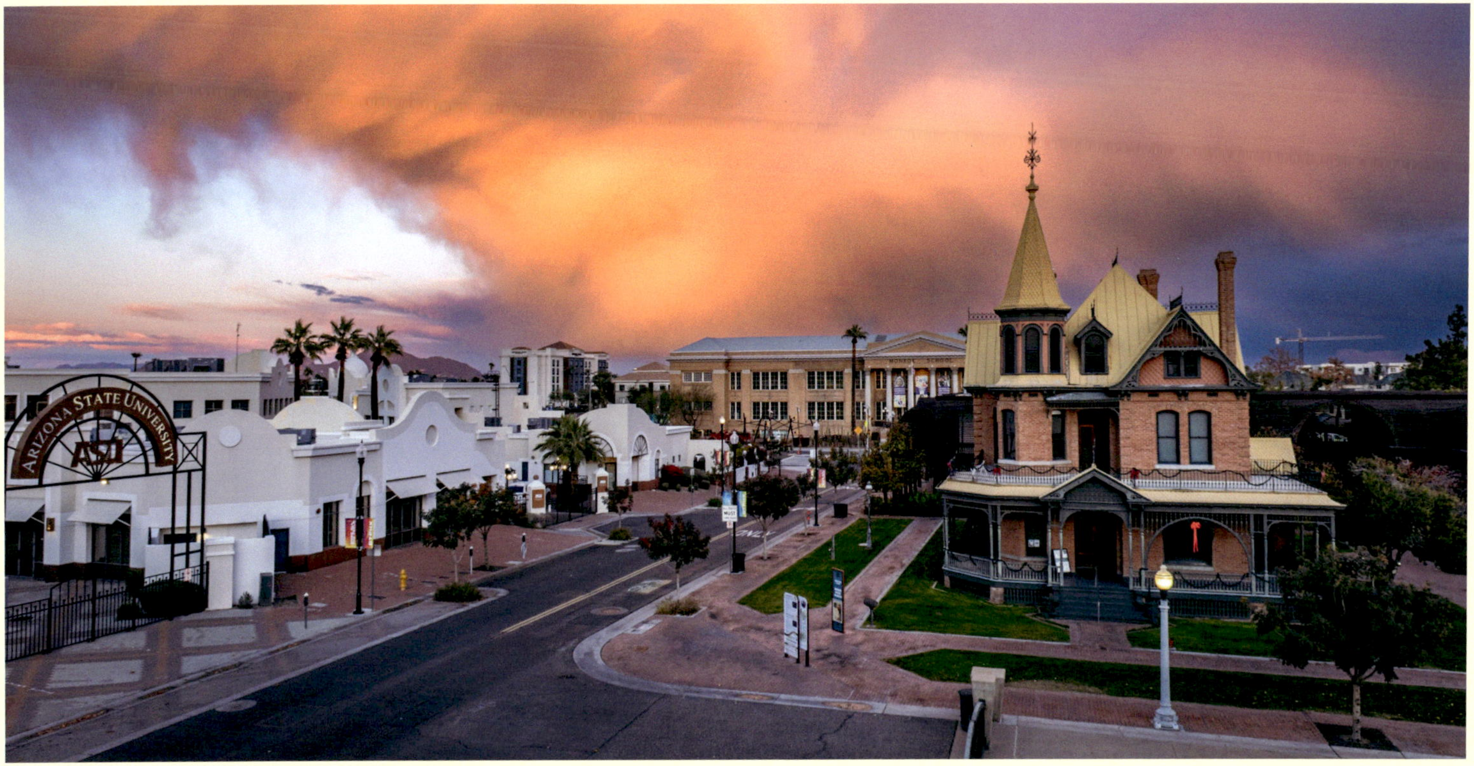

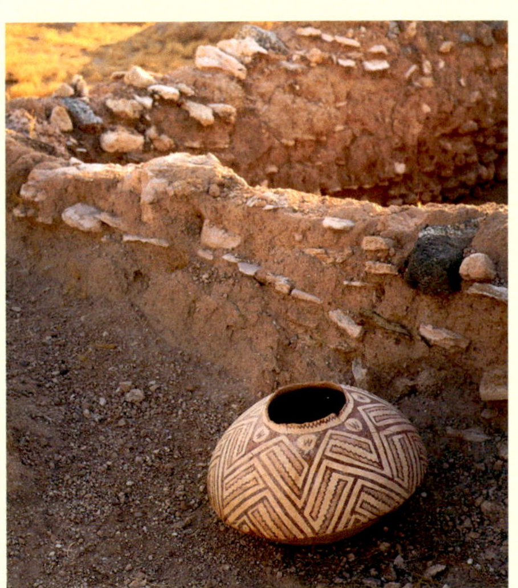

Above: Sunset illuminates the sky over the Arizona State University Mercado (left), Children's Museum of Phoenix (center), and historic Rosson House (right). JAKE CASE

Left: This large Hohokam-decorated ceramic vessel is part of a 1,500-year-old archaeological site on display at the S'edav Va'aki Museum (formerly Pueblo Grande Museum) in Phoenix. LARRY LINDAHL

Facing page, right: Cars bustle along Washington Street as dusk settles over "The Valley," as locals lovingly call the Phoenix metropolitan area. JAKE CASE

Facing page, left top: High-rise buildings tower over Arizona State University's recently completed campus in downtown Phoenix. JAKE CASE

Facing page, left bottom: A quiet, drizzly morning greets 2nd Street by the Herberger Theatre—built in 1989 as a key piece to downtown Phoenix's revitalization. JAKE CASE

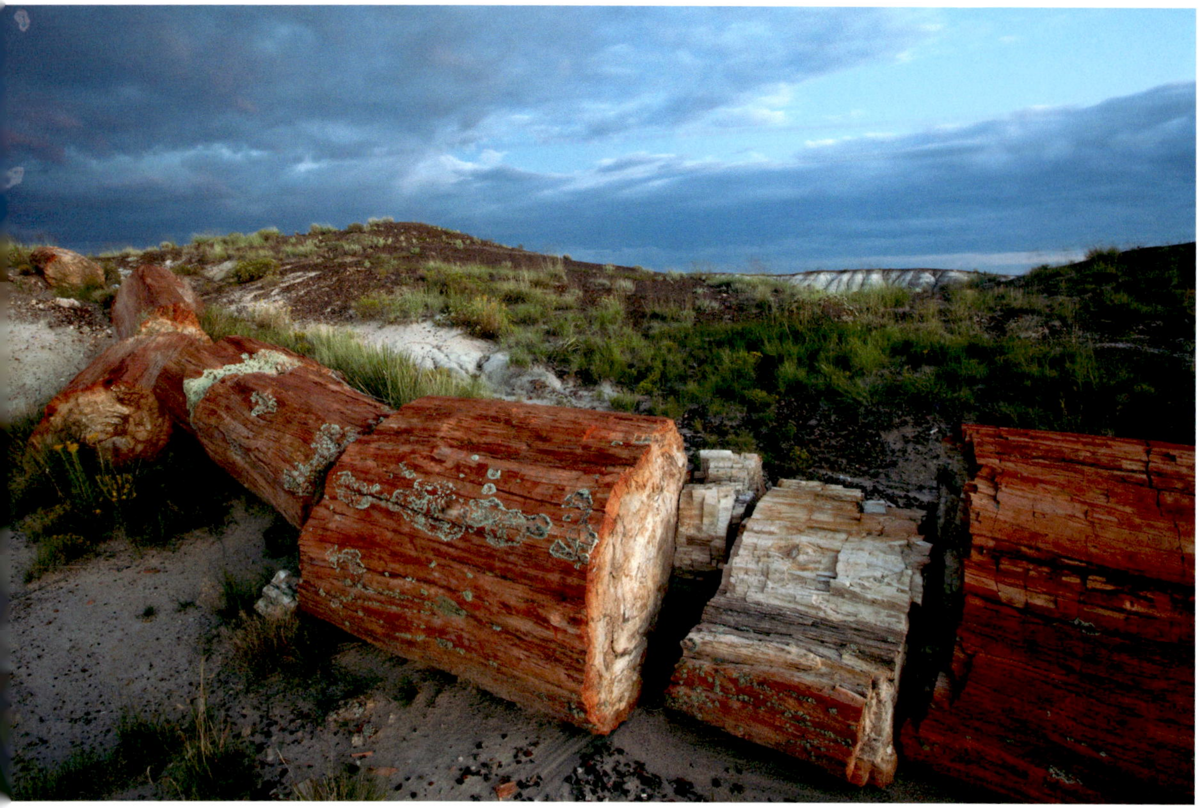

Above: Fossilized trees line the Crystal Forest Trail in Petrified Forest National Park. LARRY LINDAHL

Right: These petroglyphs were carved by occupants of the nearby Puerco Ruins, a 100-room pueblo built more than 600 years ago, now part of Petrified Forest National Park. LARRY LINDAHL

Far right: A spring storm passes over Watson Lake near Prescott. The boulder-strewn backdrop—known as the Granite Dells—were formed about 1.4 billion years ago. JAKE CASE

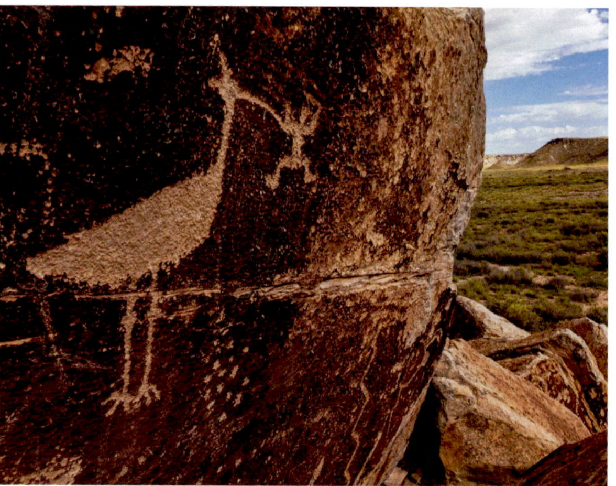

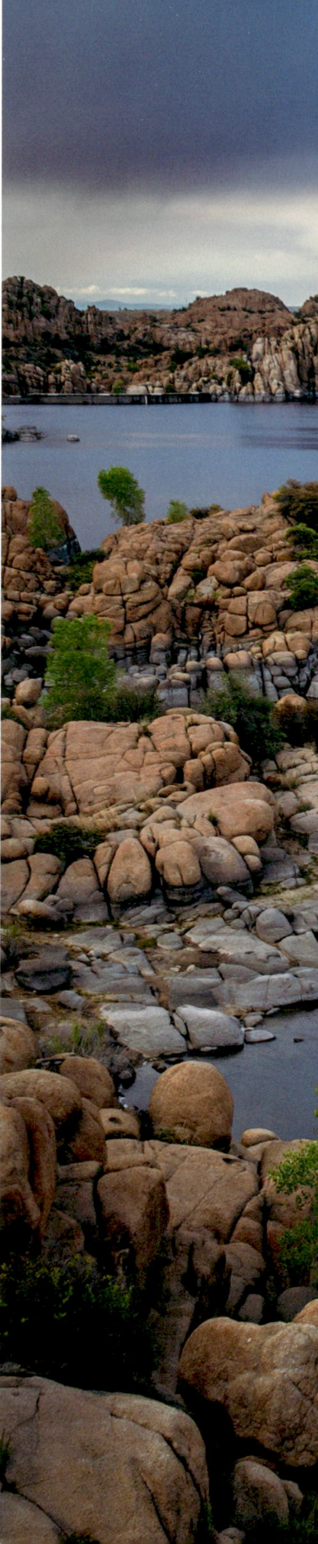

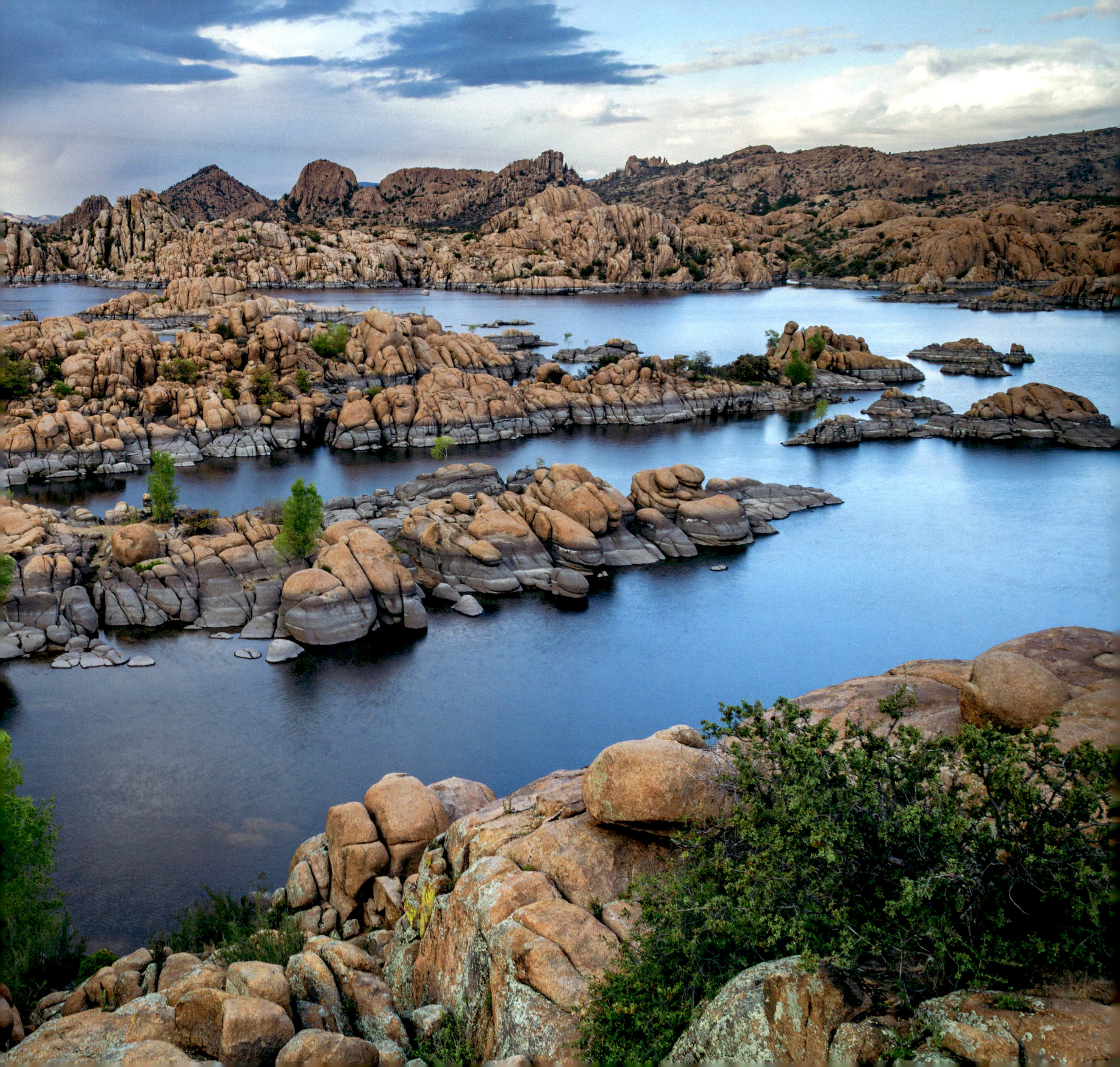

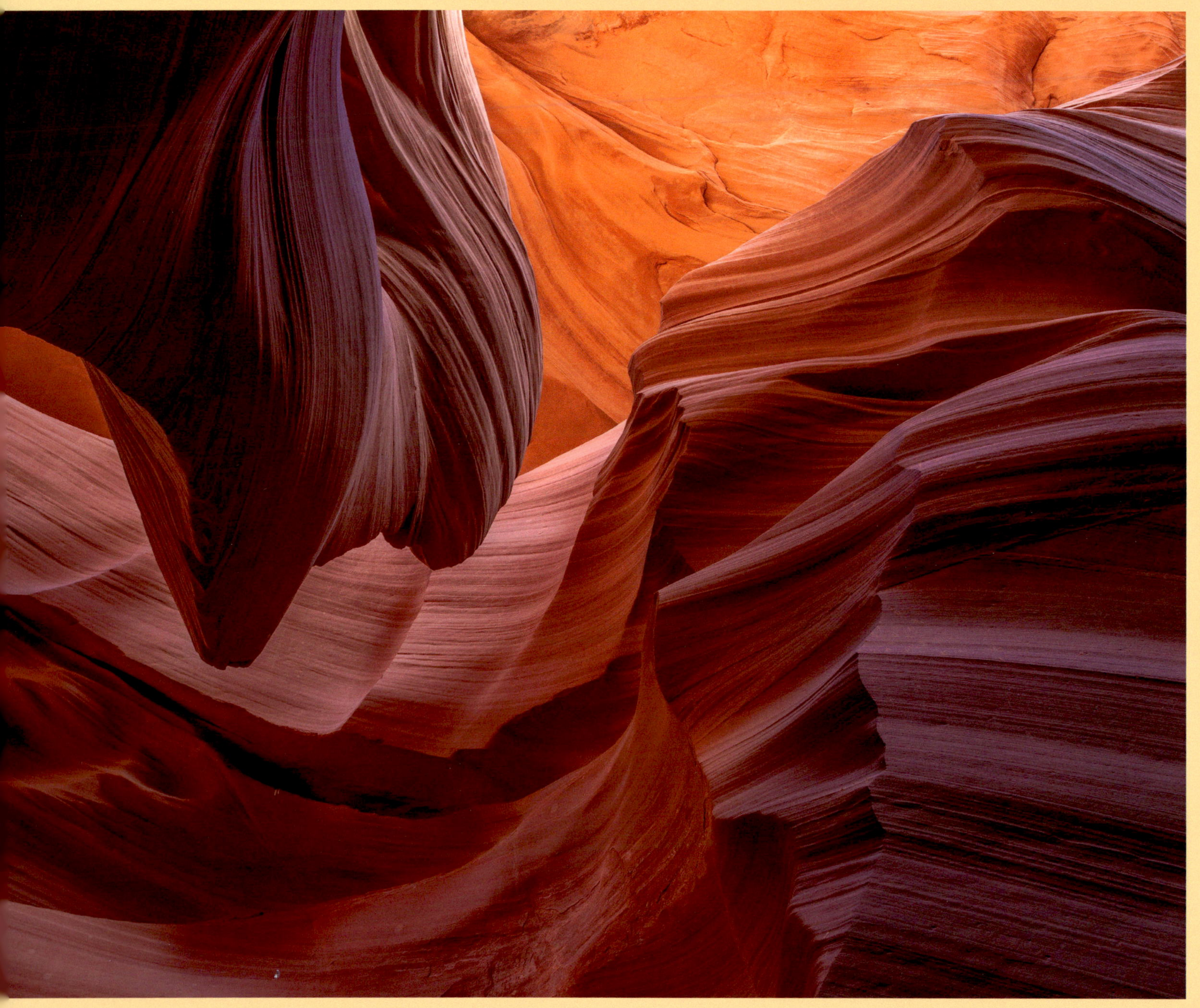

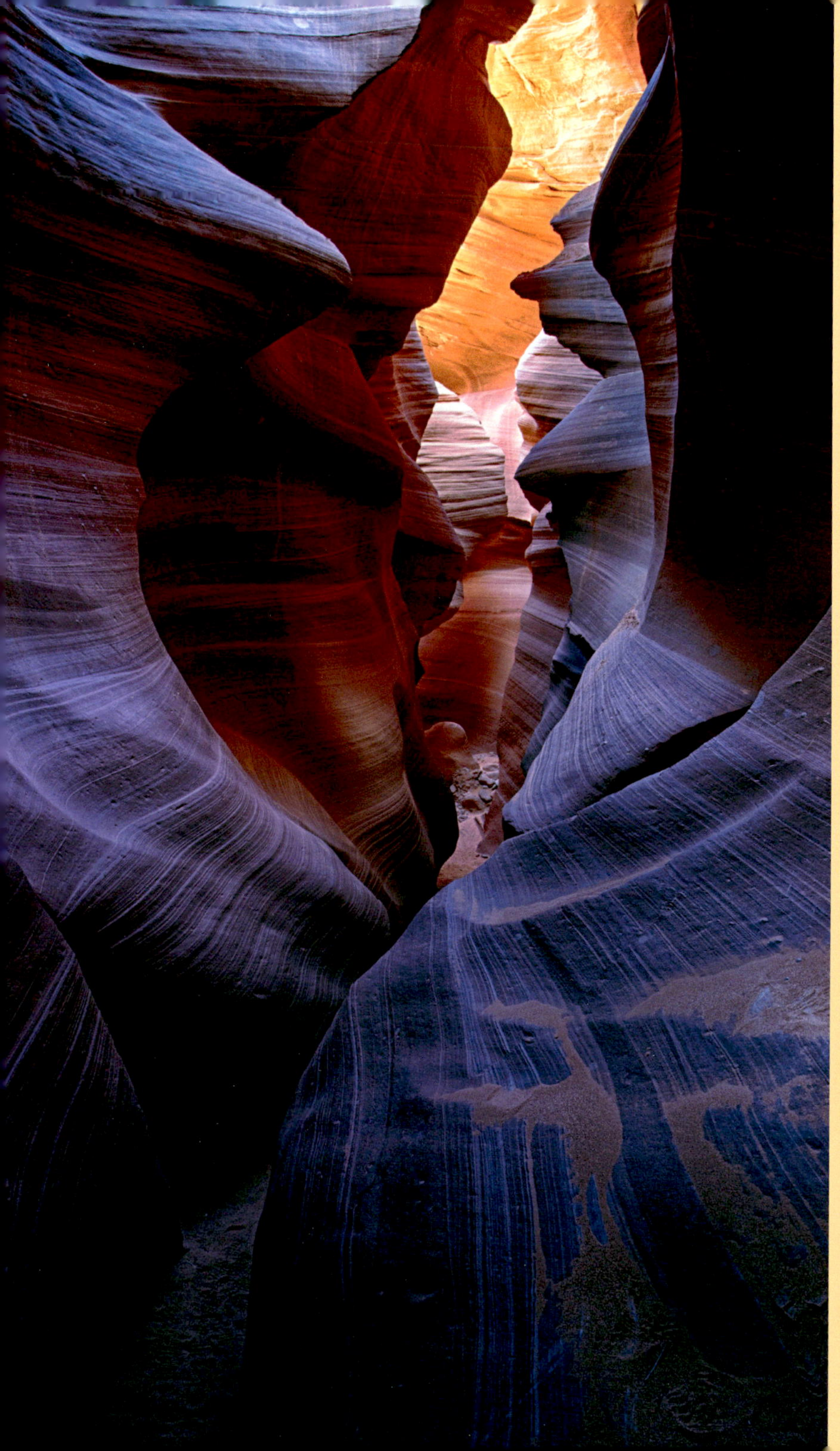

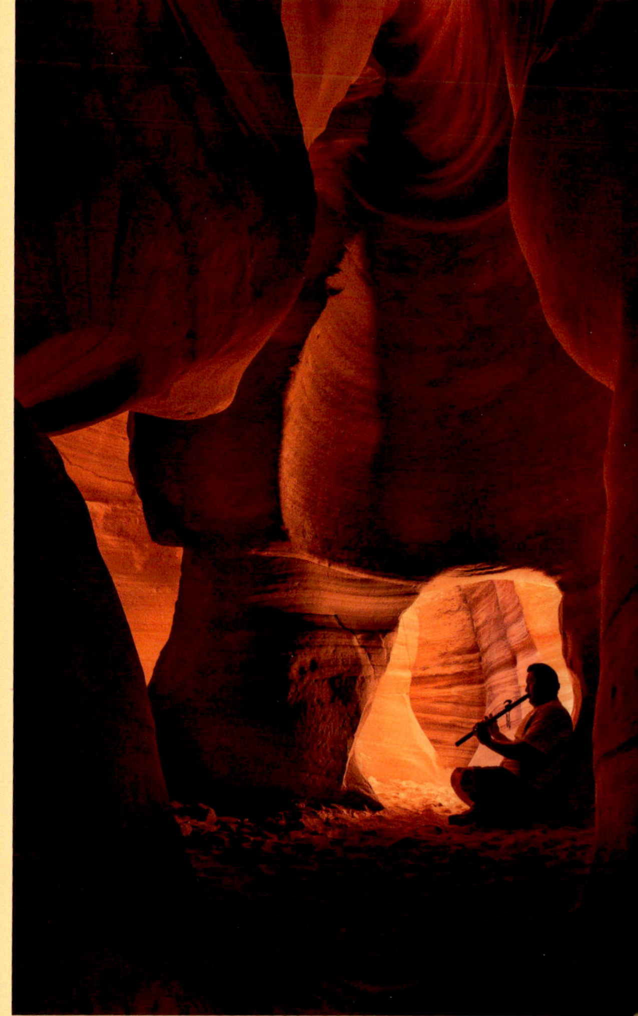

Above: A Navajo guide plays his cedar flute, the music softly echoing in Canyon X, near Page. LARRY LINDAHL

Left and facing page: Water-swept erosion carves other-worldly shapes from the soft Navajo Sandstone in Antelope Canyon. LARRY LINDAHL

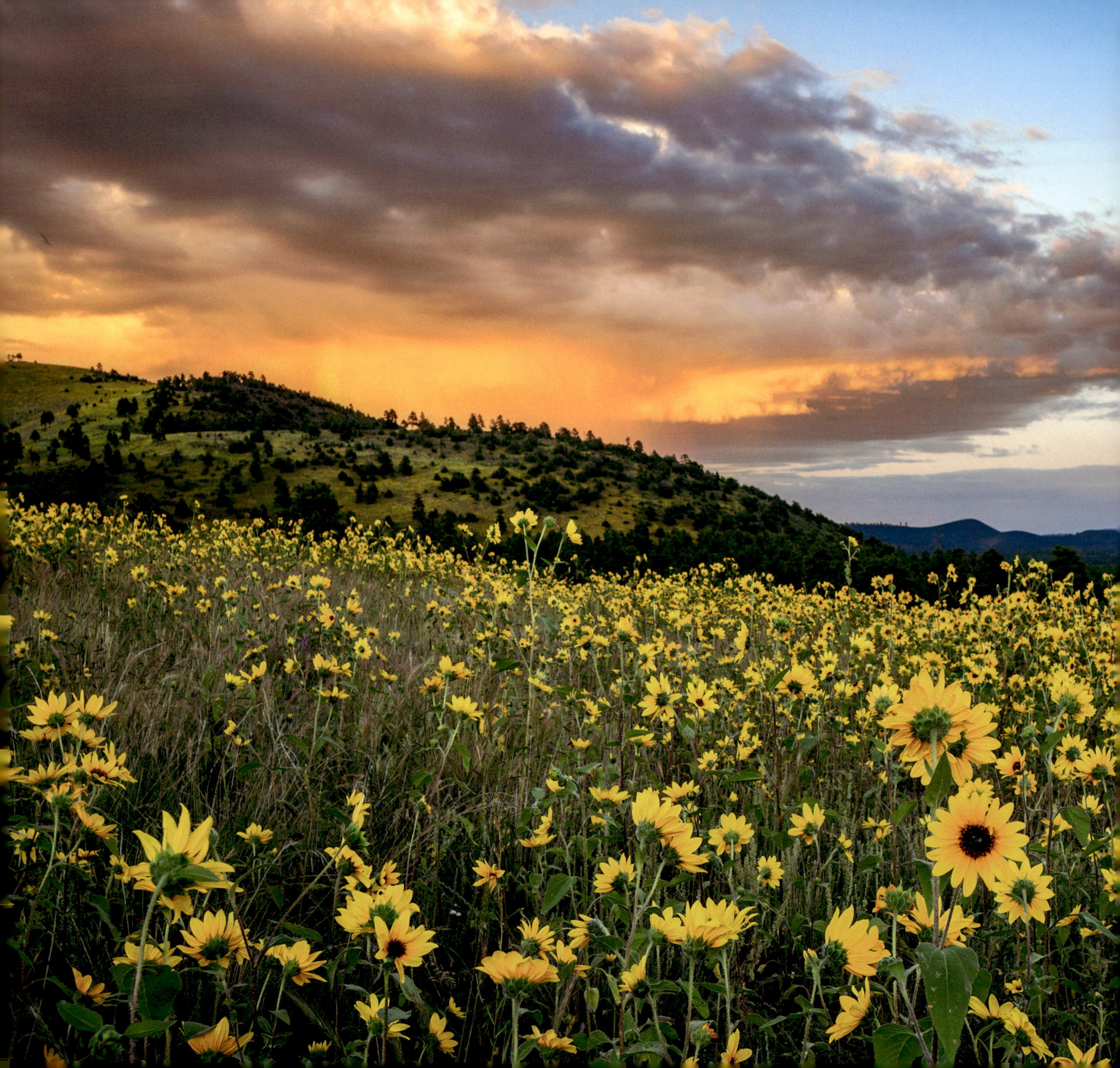

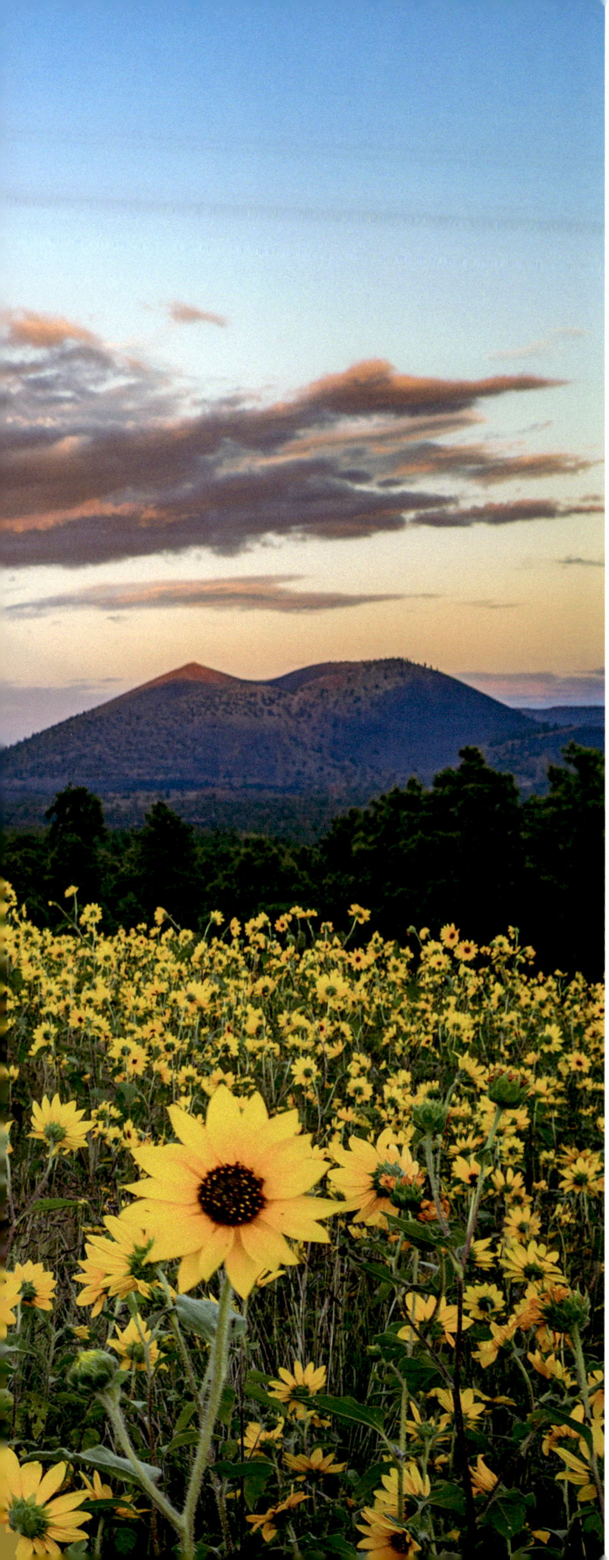

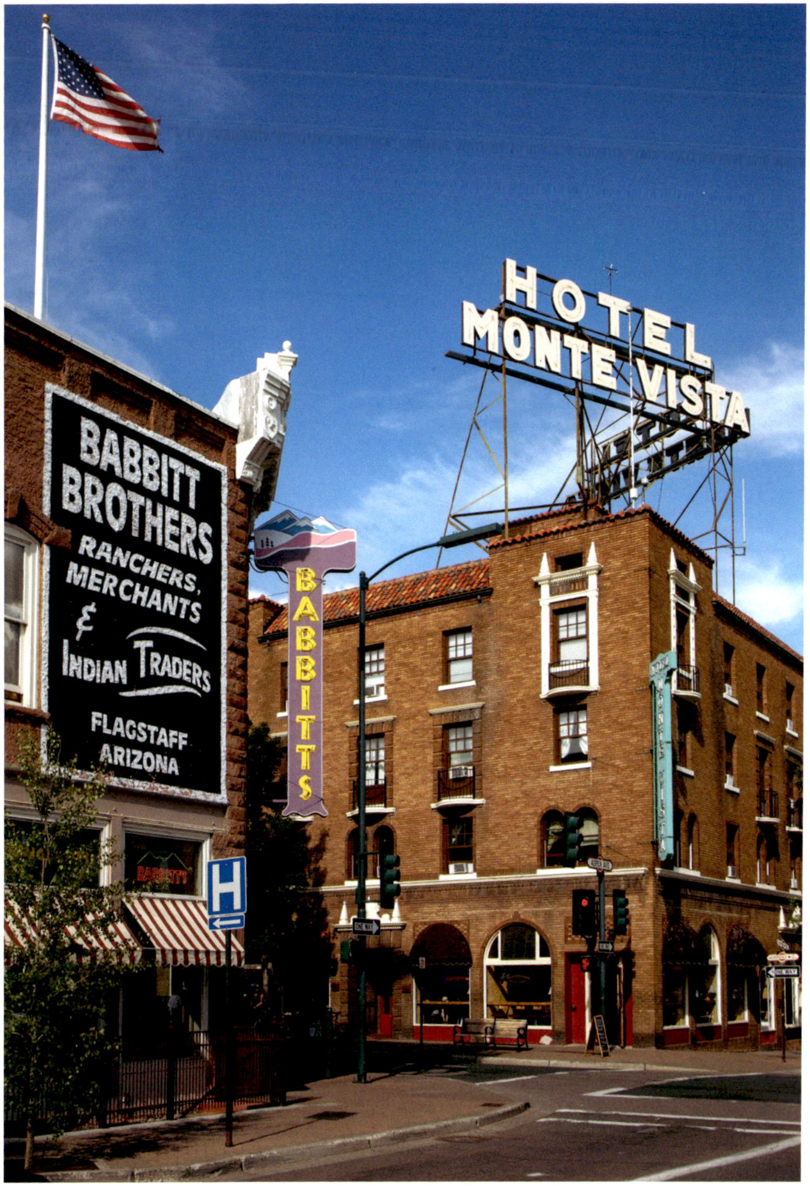

Above: With its ornate brickwork and red tile roof, Hotel Monte Vista, built in 1927, is the centerpiece of Flagstaff's Old Town district. LARRY LINDAHL

Left: Monsoon season's summer rains bring stunning sunsets and sunflower blooms to Sunset Crater Volcano National Monument. JAKE CASE

Right: Window Rock or Tséghánoodzání frames a monument to the Navajo Code Talkers of WW II in Navajo Tribal Park. LARRY LINDAHL

Far right: In the late-1200s, Keet Seel housed up to 150 residents. The Ancestral Puebloan site in Navajo National Monument is accessible only by an overnight, 17-mile roundtrip hike. LARRY LINDAHL

Below: Mummy Cave, with nearly 70 rooms, is the largest ancient dwelling in Canyon de Chelly National Monument. LARRY LINDAHL

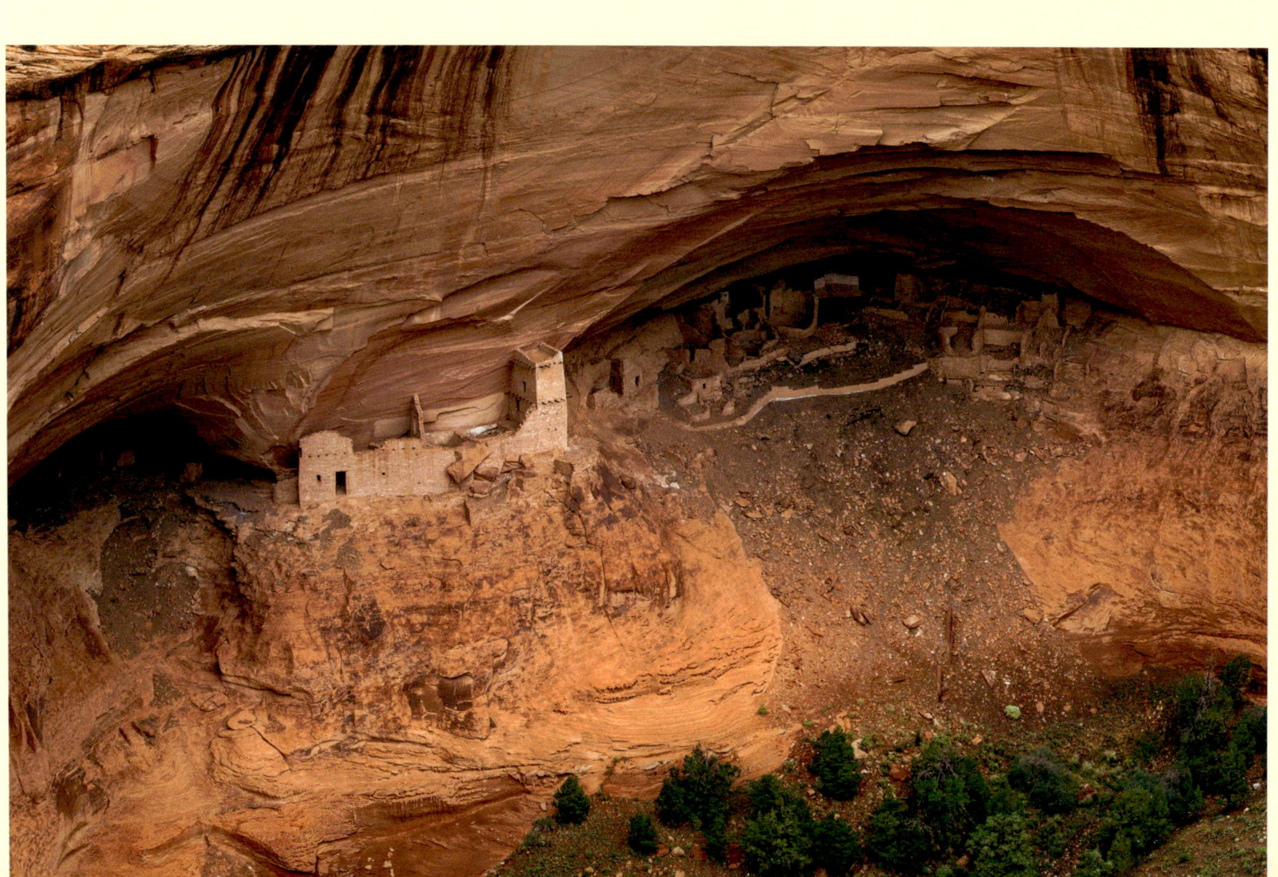

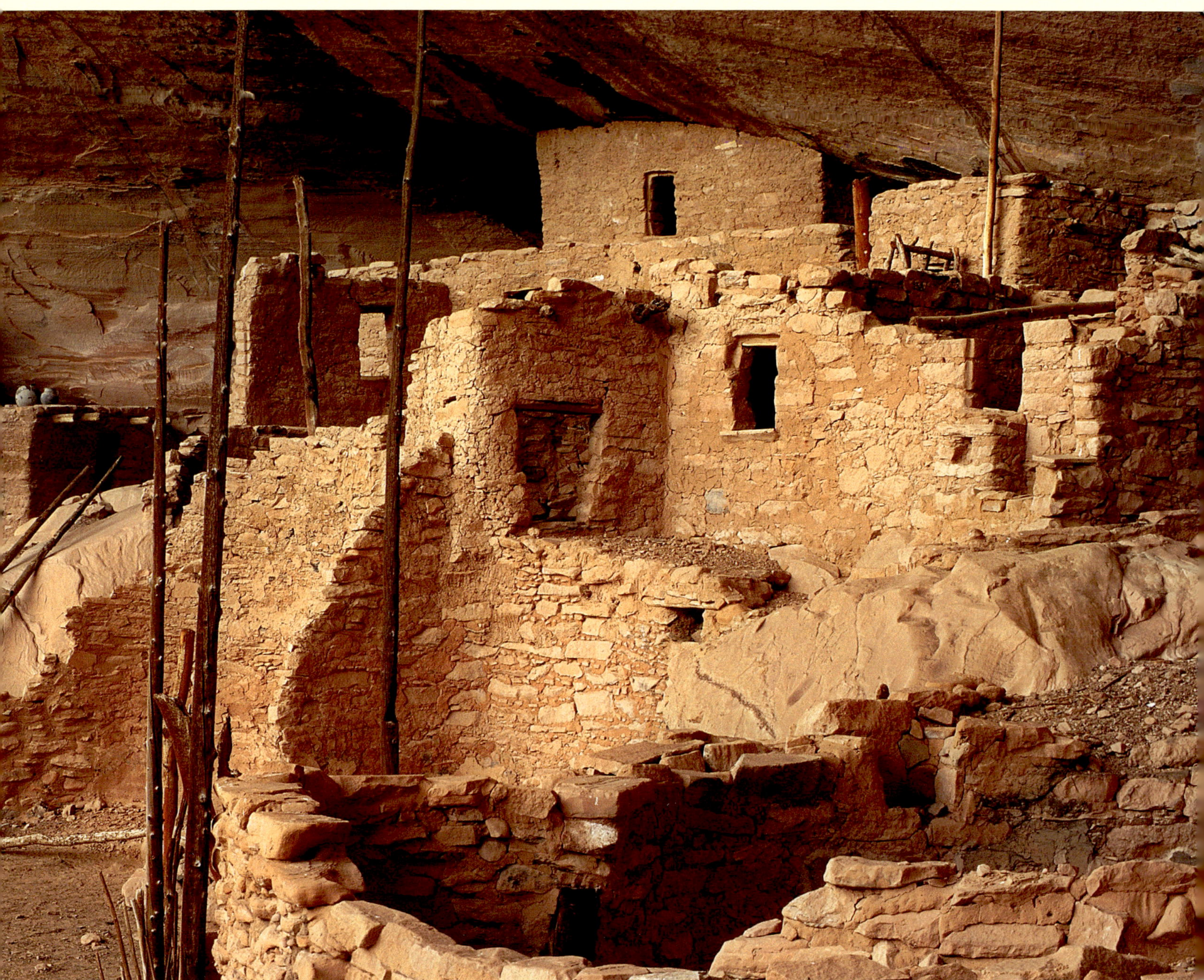

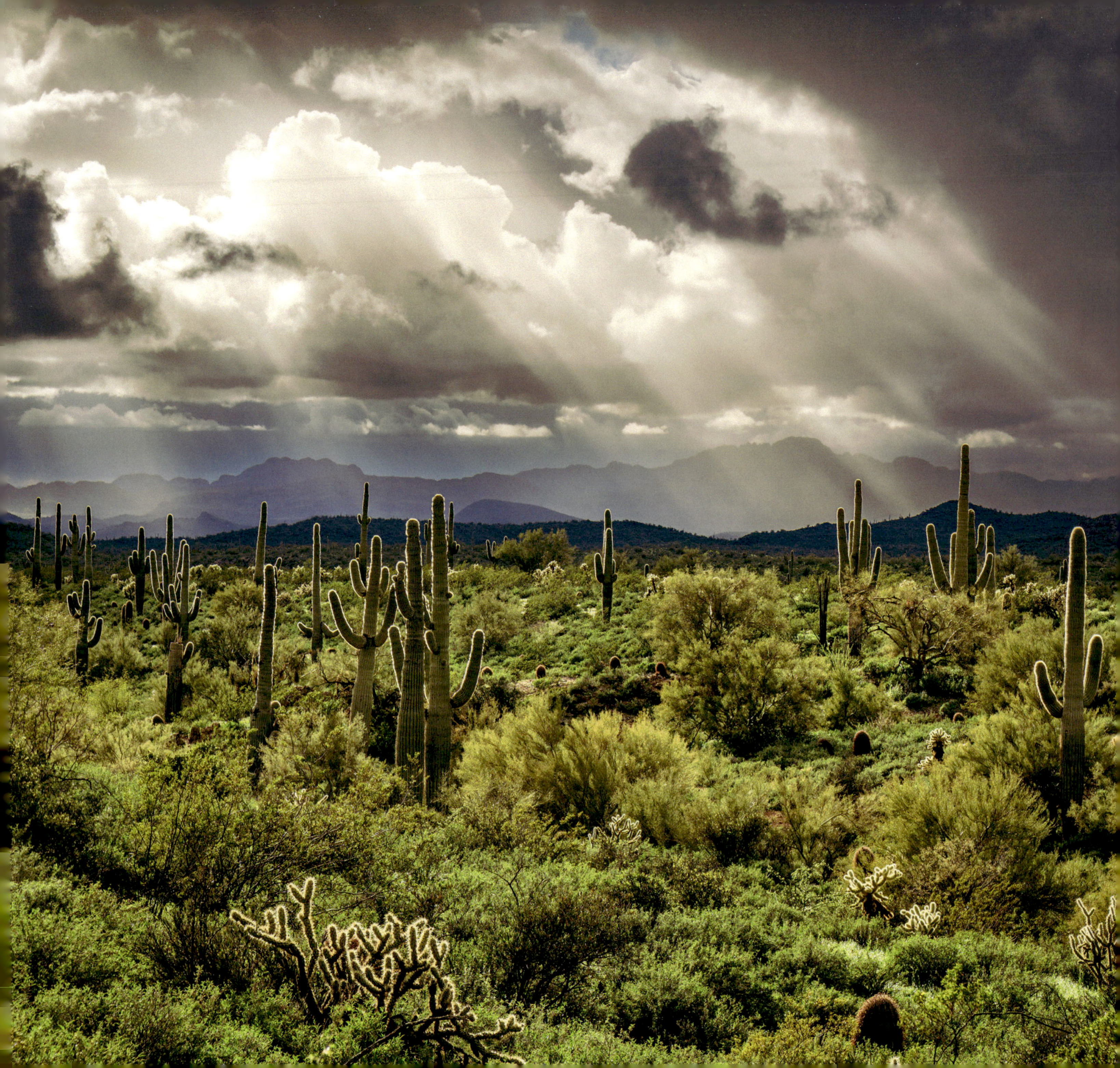

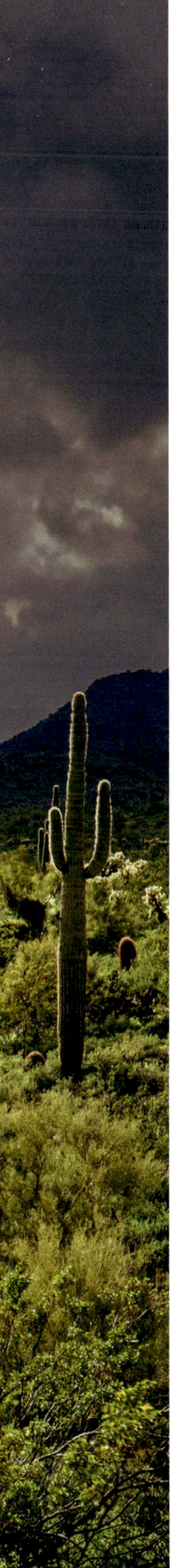

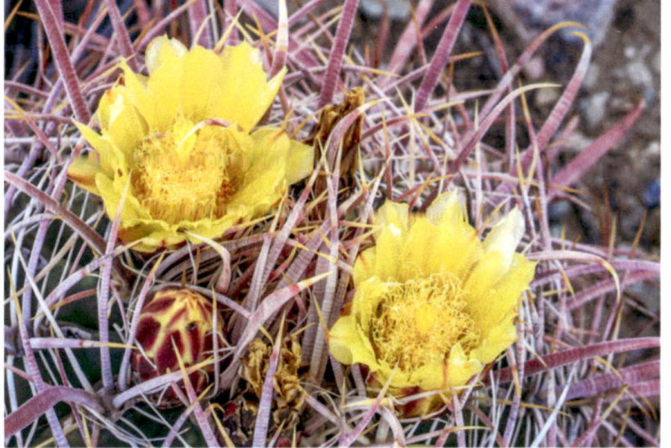

Left: March and April bring cactus flowers to the Sonoran Desert, like this duo sprung from a fishhook barrel cactus. JAKE CASE

Far left: Sunbeams break through a winter storm over the Hieroglyphic Mountains as seasonal rains quench this arid region. JAKE CASE

Below: Saguaros, palo verde trees, and ocotillos bask in the radiance of golden hour in the Vulture Mountains near Wickenburg. JAKE CASE

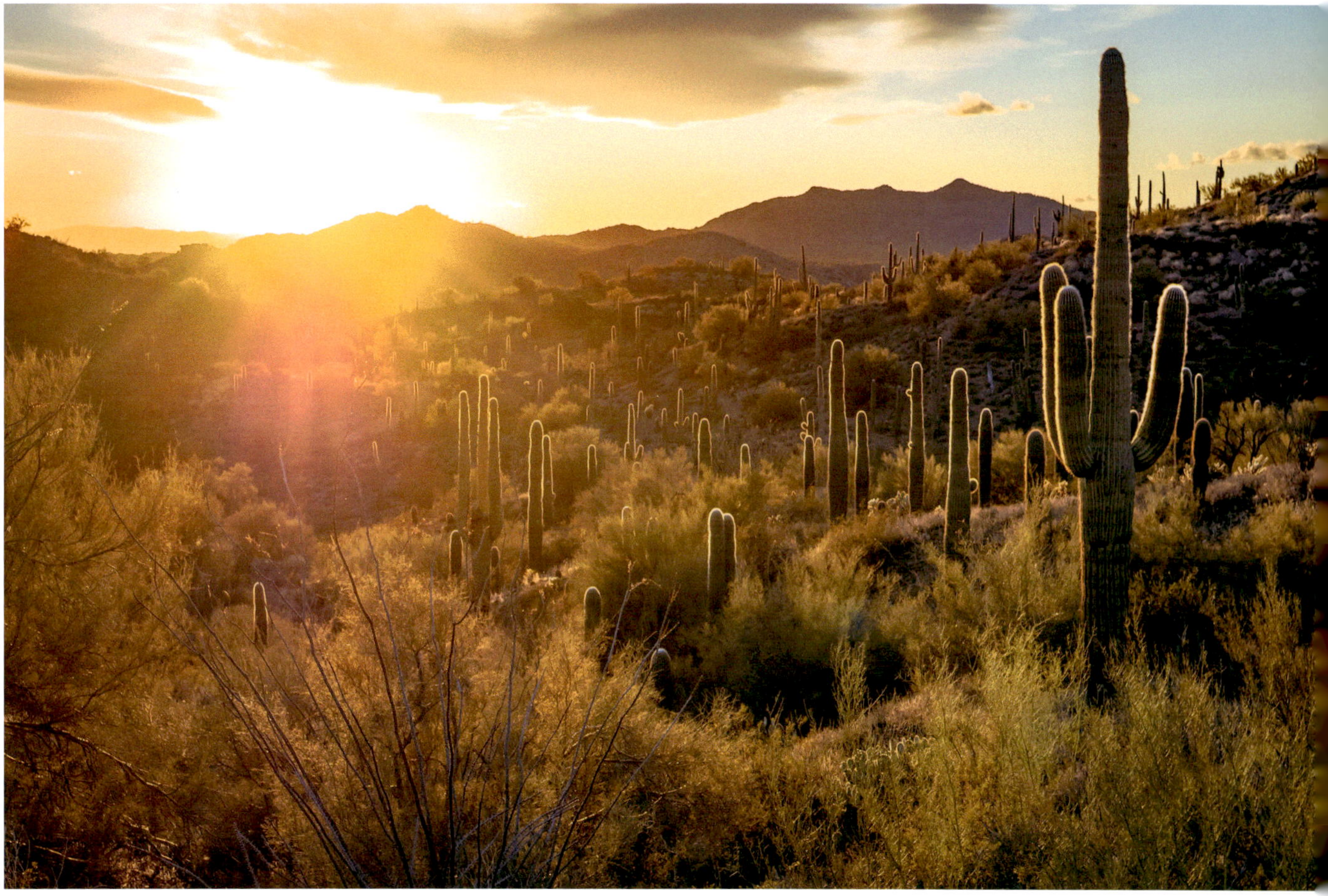

Right: Celebrated in Prescott since 1888, the World's Oldest Rodeo opens with the Grand Entry flag presentation. LARRY LINDAHL

Far right: The Kayenta 4th of July Rodeo, hosted by the town of about 5,000 residents, draws participants from across the vast Navajo Nation. LARRY LINDAHL

Below: Steer wrestling is a popular event at the World's Oldest Rodeo in Prescott. LARRY LINDAHL

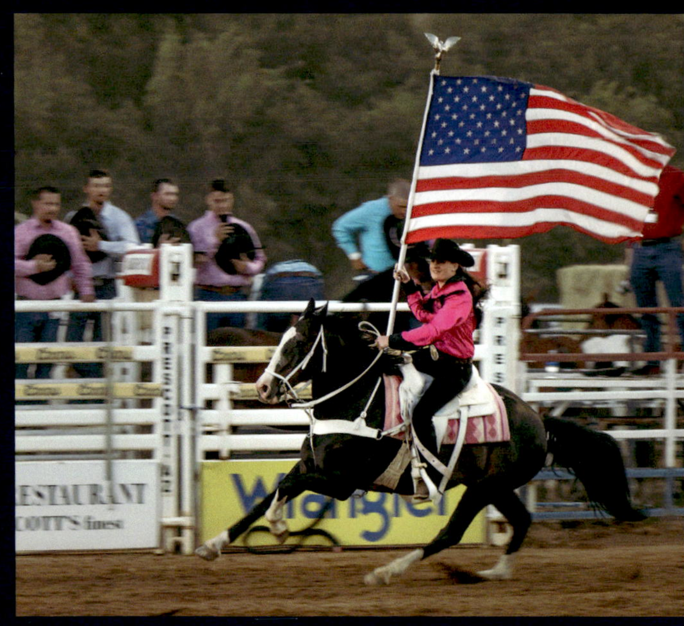

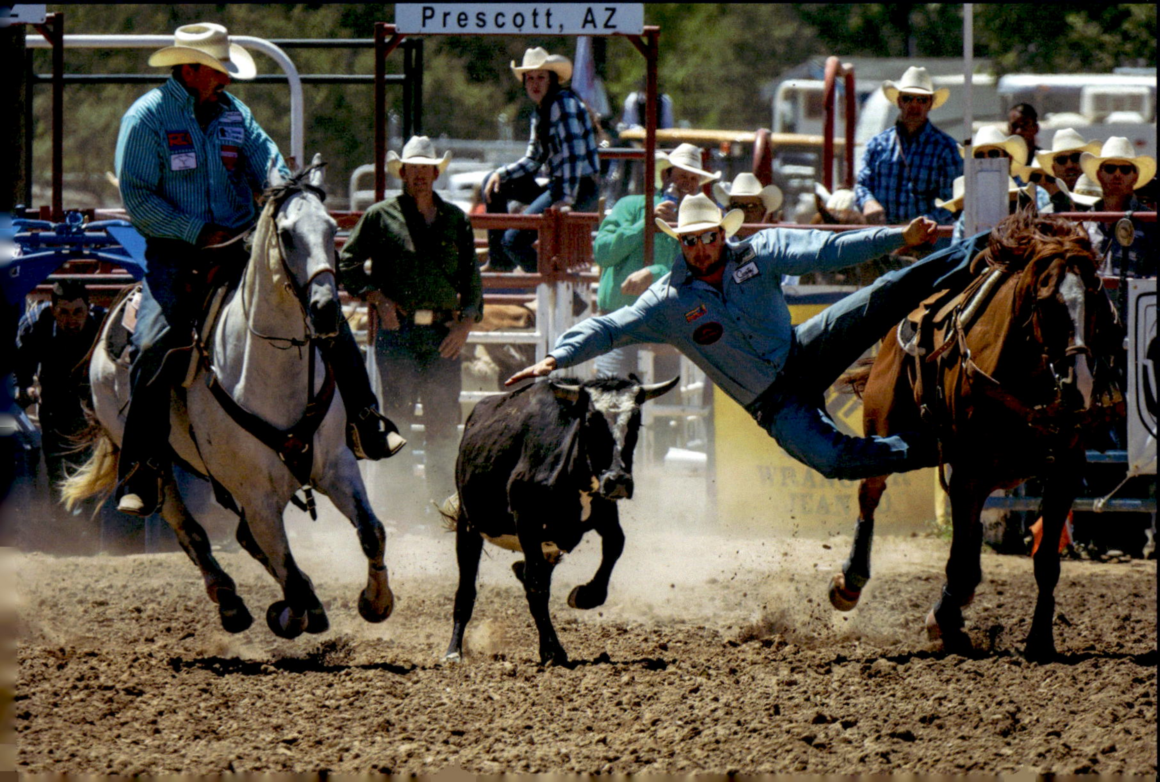

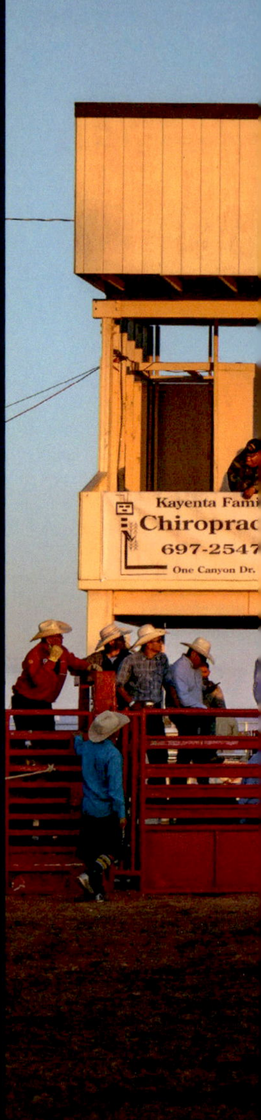

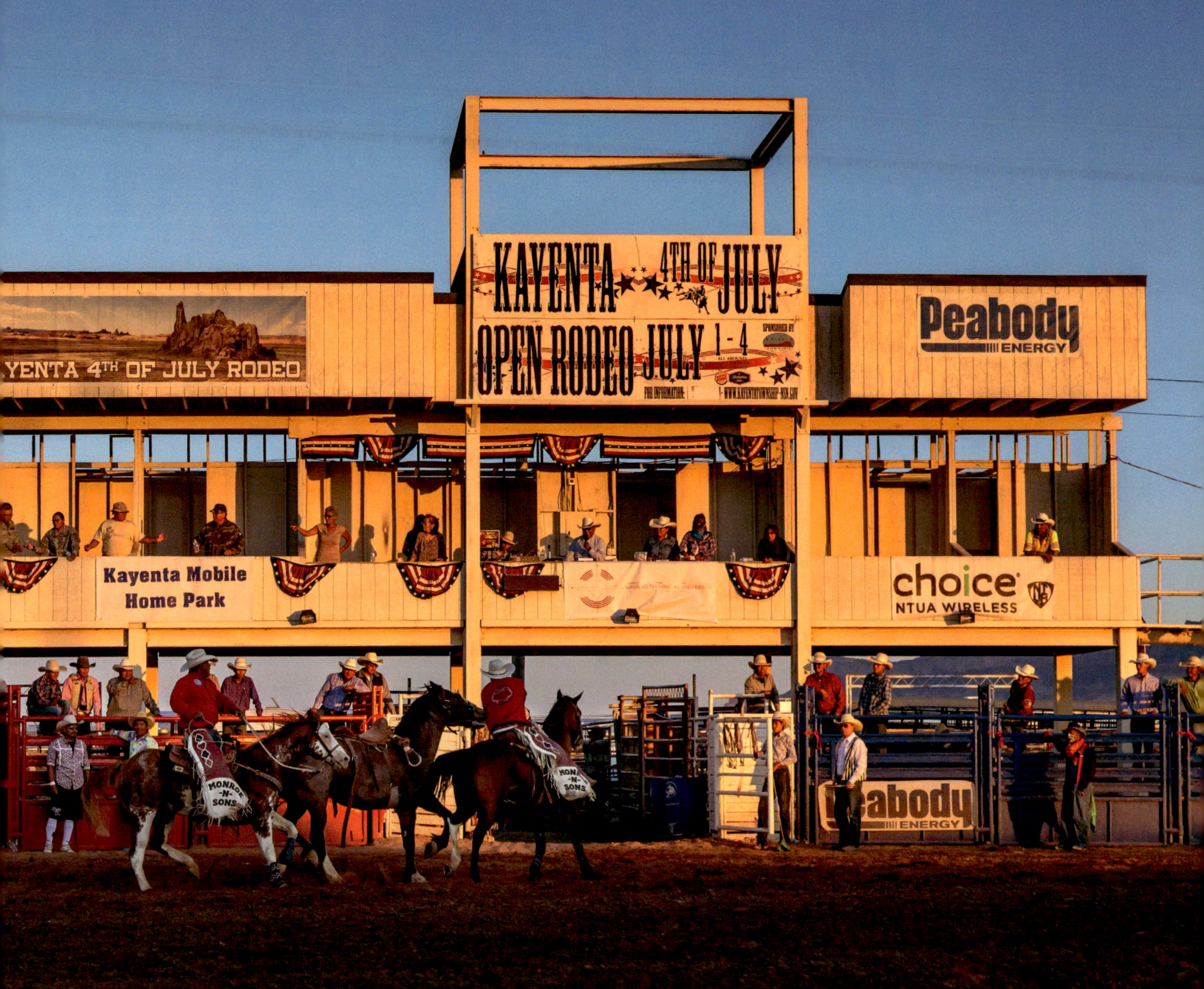
YENTA 4TH OF JULY RODEO
KAYENTA 4TH OF JULY
OPEN RODEO JULY 1-4
Peabody ENERGY
Kayenta Mobile Home Park
choice NTUA WIRELESS
MONROE -N- SONS
MONROE -N- SONS
Peabody ENERGY

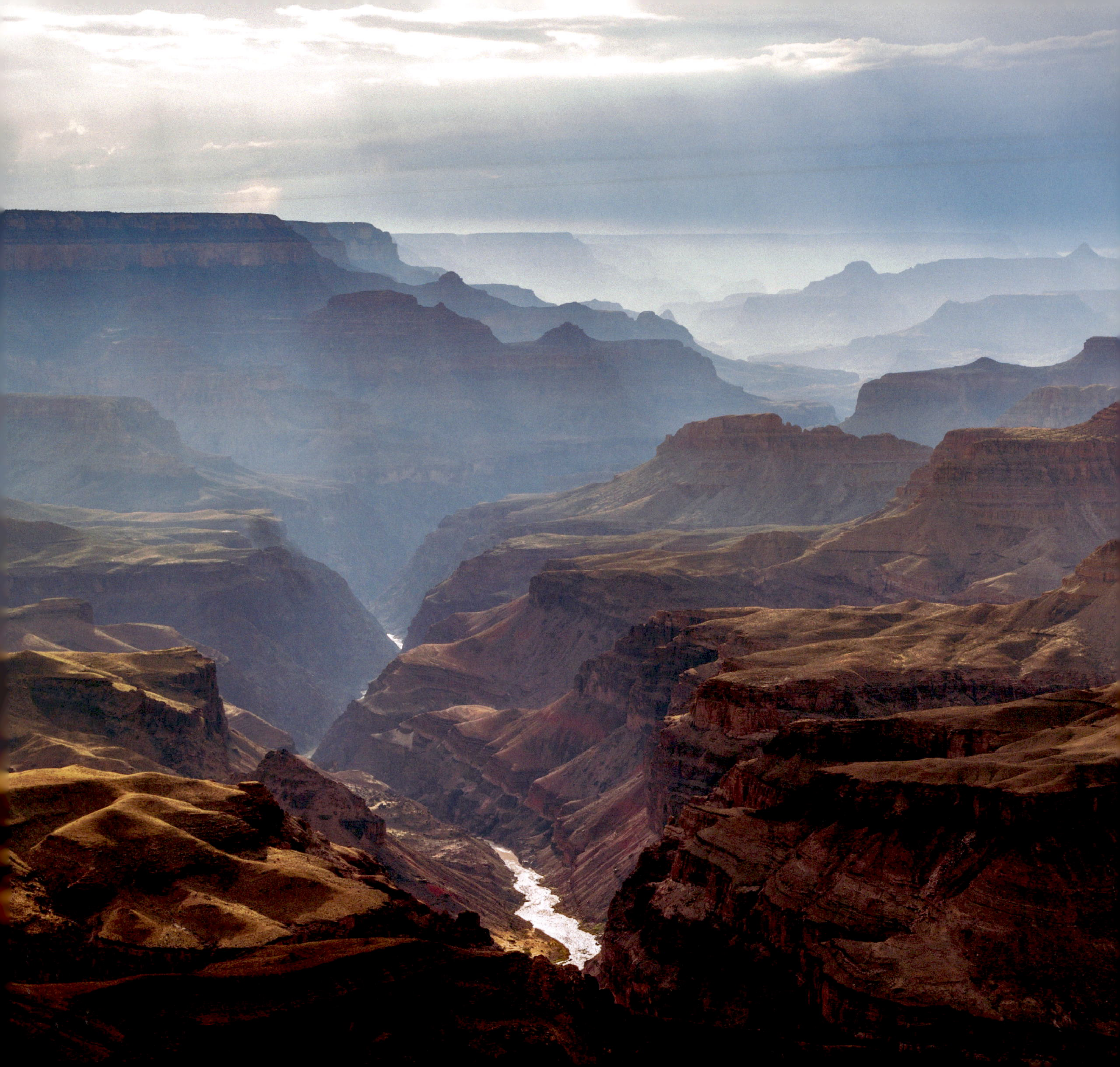

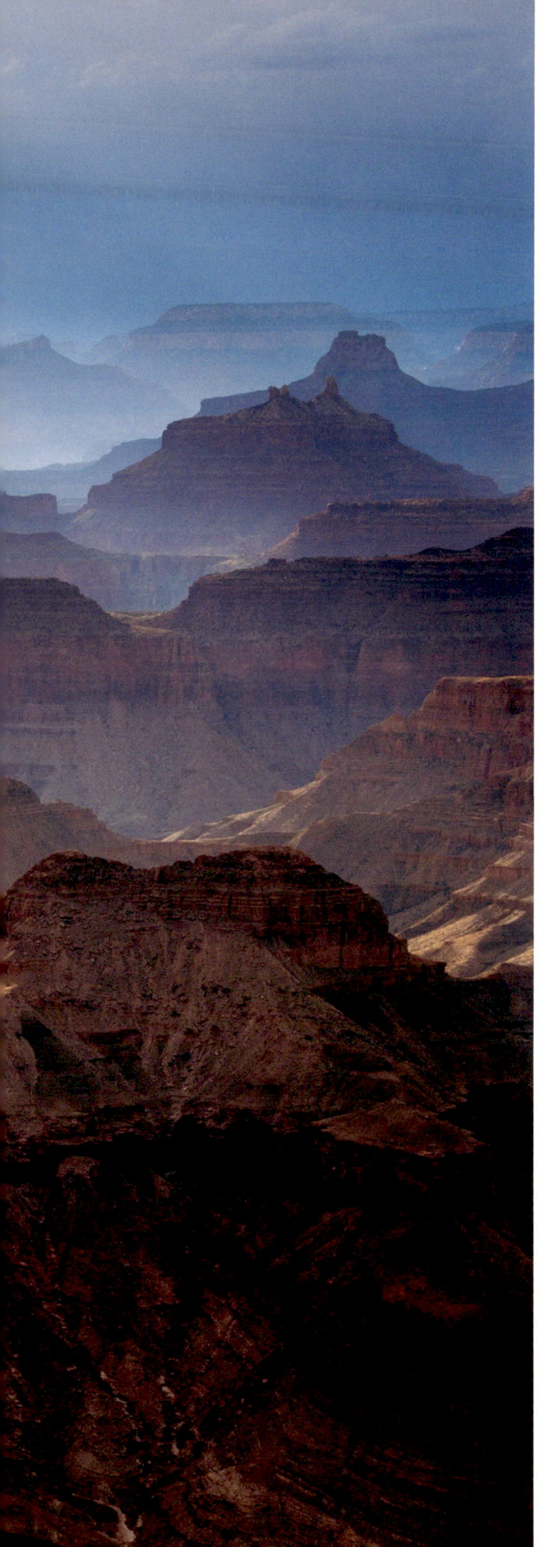

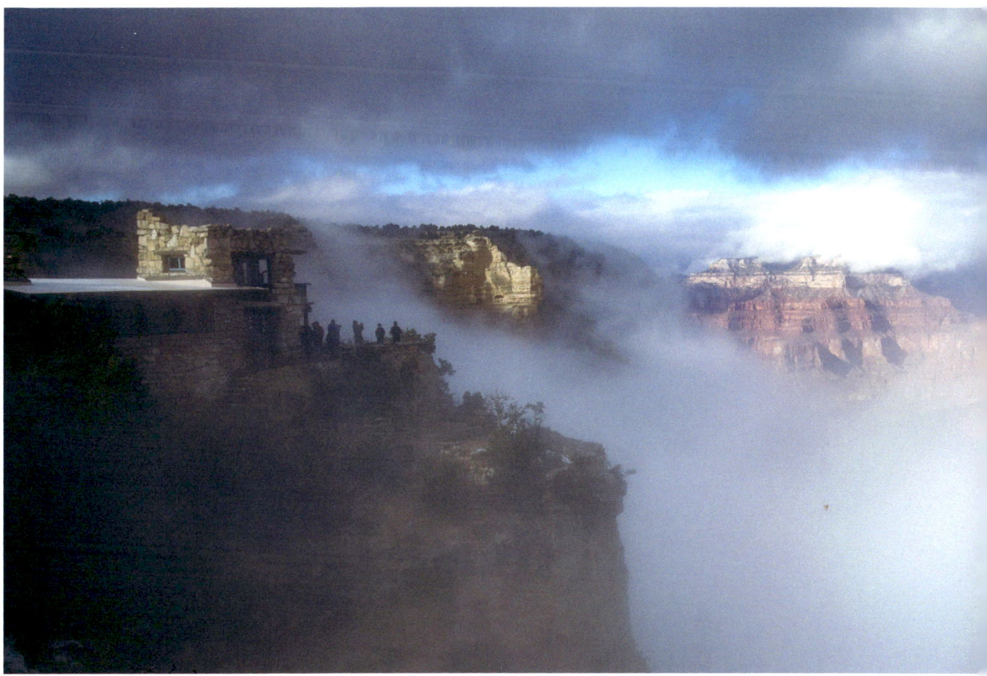

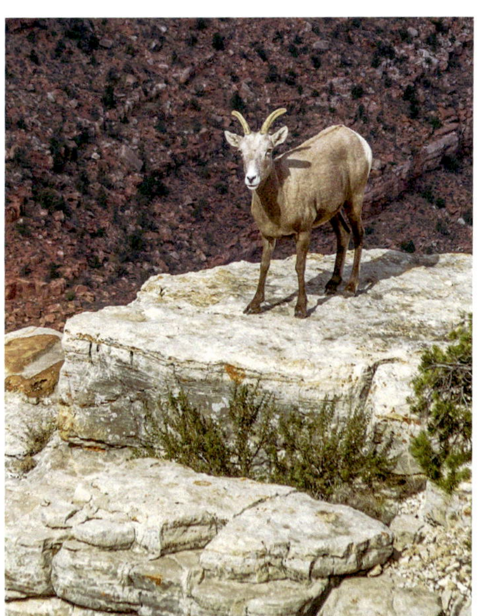

Above: Fog shrouds much of the Grand Canyon as visitors look on from the balcony of Lookout Studio, designed by architect Mary Coulter and built by the Fred Harvey Company in 1914. JAKE CASE

Left: A juvenile male desert bighorn sheep stands on a 260-million-year-old limestone ledge at the Grand Canyon South Rim. JAKE CASE

Far left: Far below Lipan Point, the Colorado River roars through Hance Rapid in the maze of the Grand Canyon. JAKE CASE

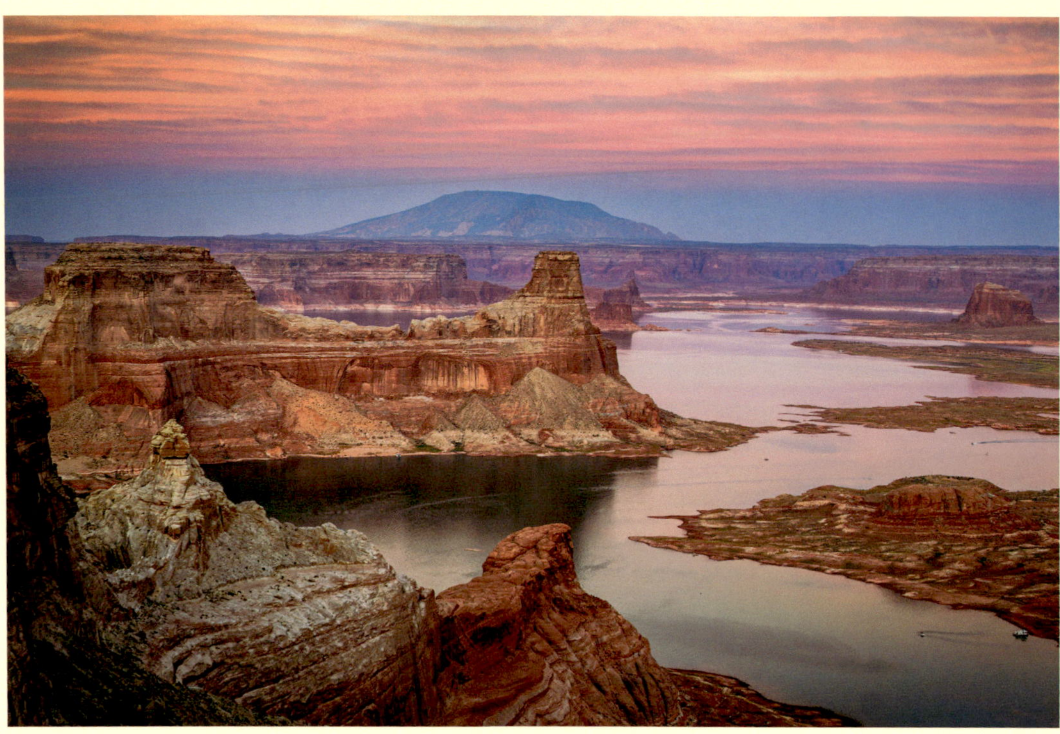

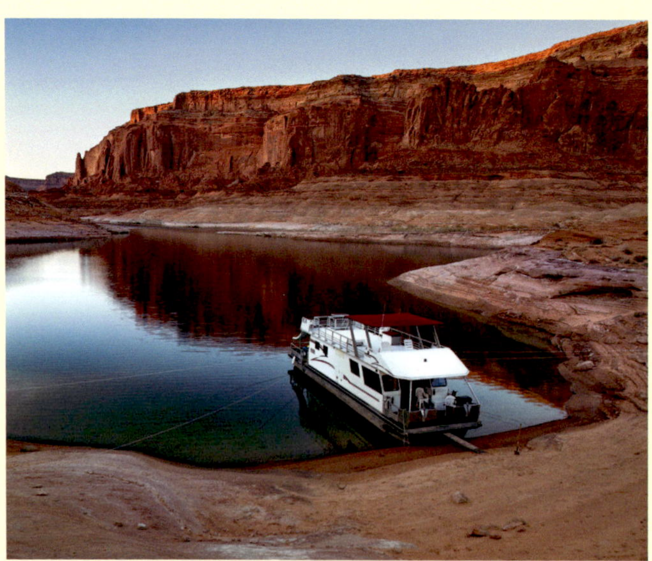

Above: Gunsight Butte stands prominently over Lake Powell, while Navajo Mountain's hulking profile looms on the eastern horizon, as viewed from Alstrom Point. JAKE CASE

Right: A houseboat moors in a sheltered cove on Lake Powell in Glen Canyon National Recreation Area. LARRY LINDAHL

Far right: A monsoon sunset enflames the sky over a small side canyon in Glen Canyon National Recreation Area. JAKE CASE

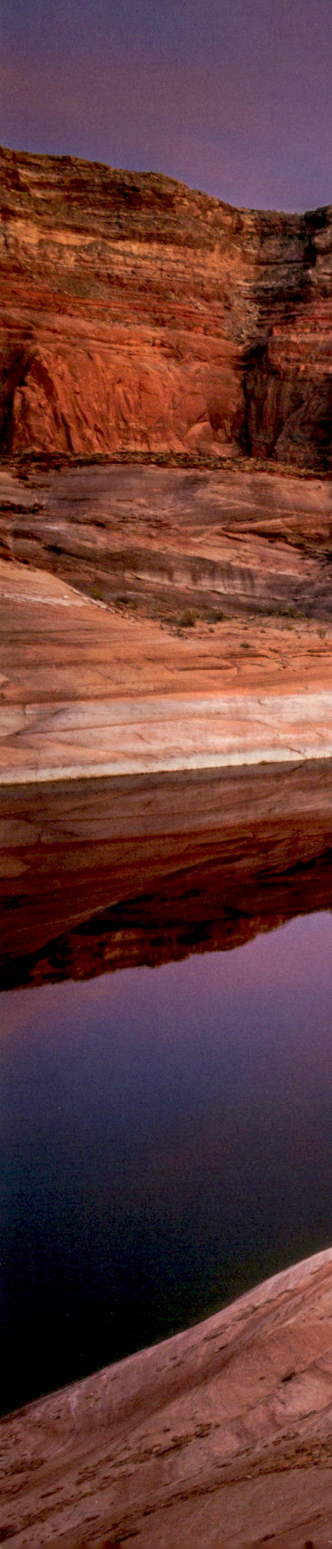

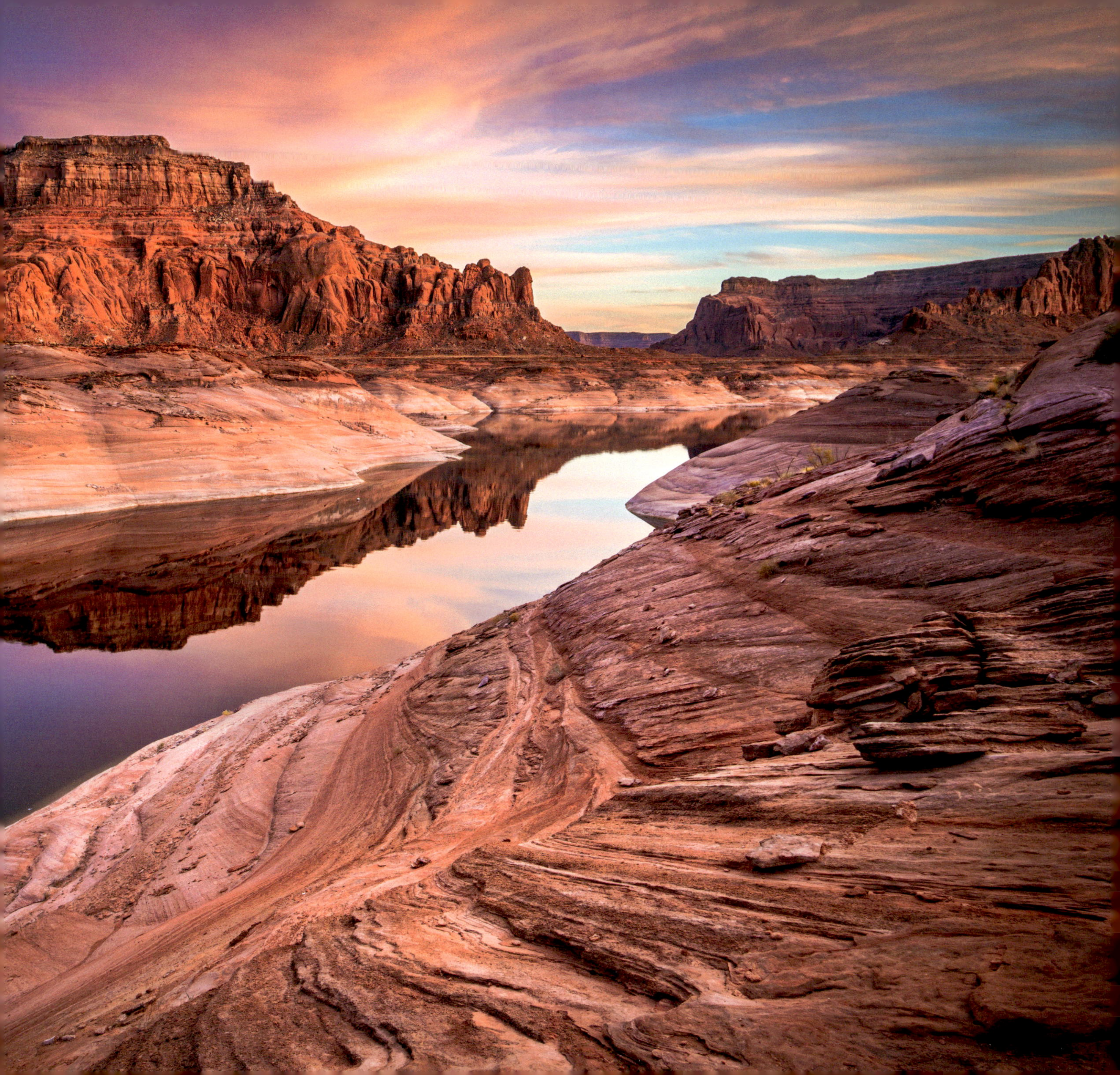

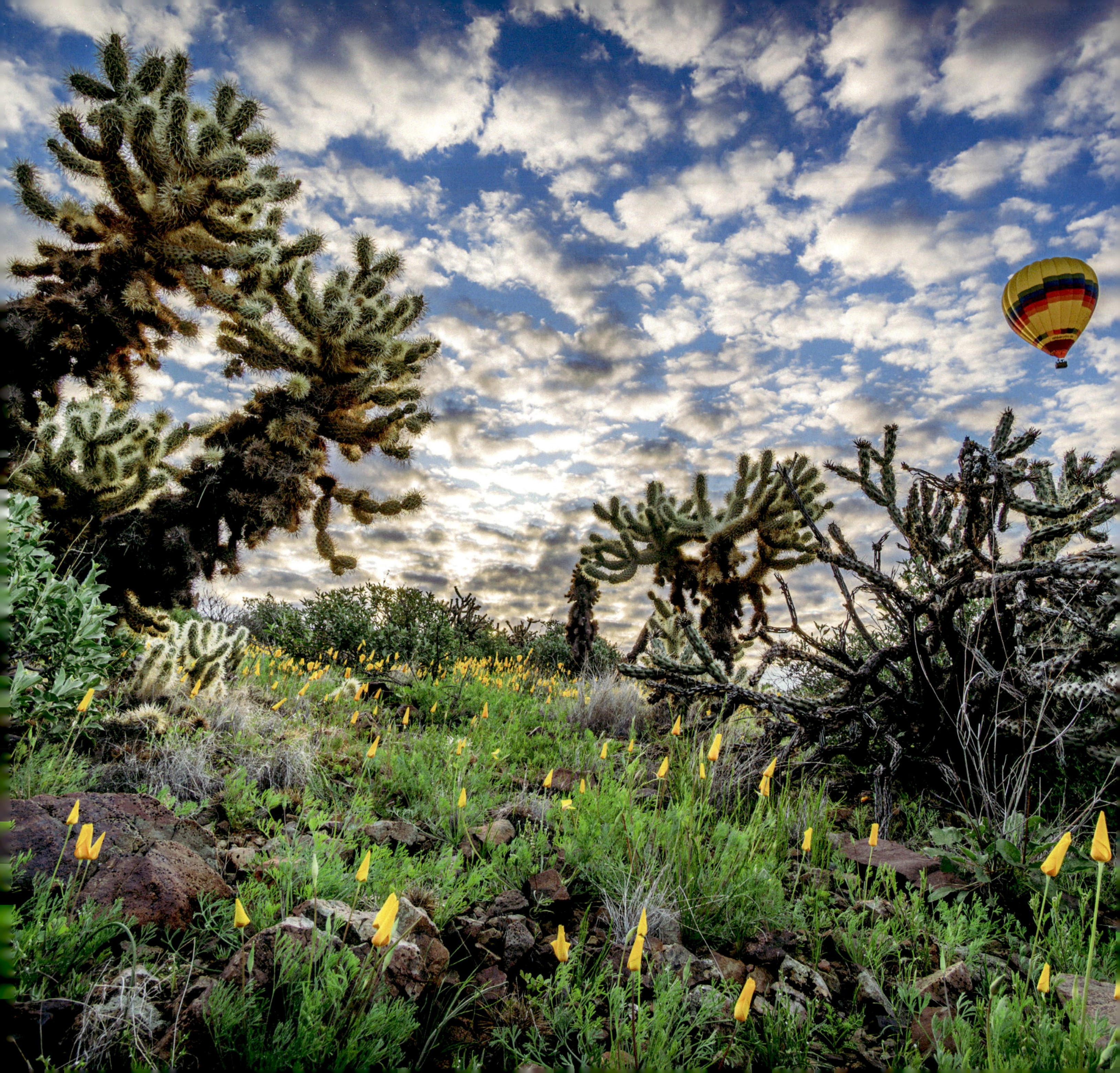

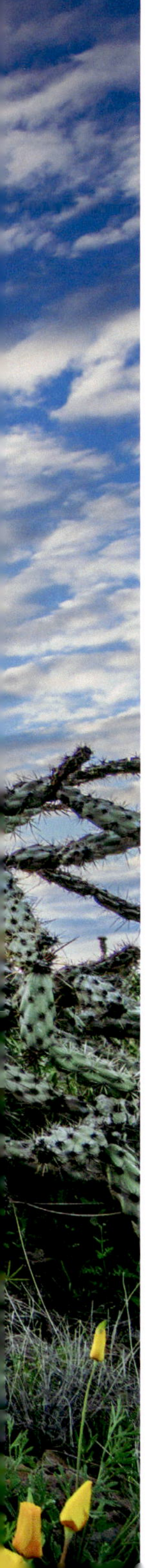

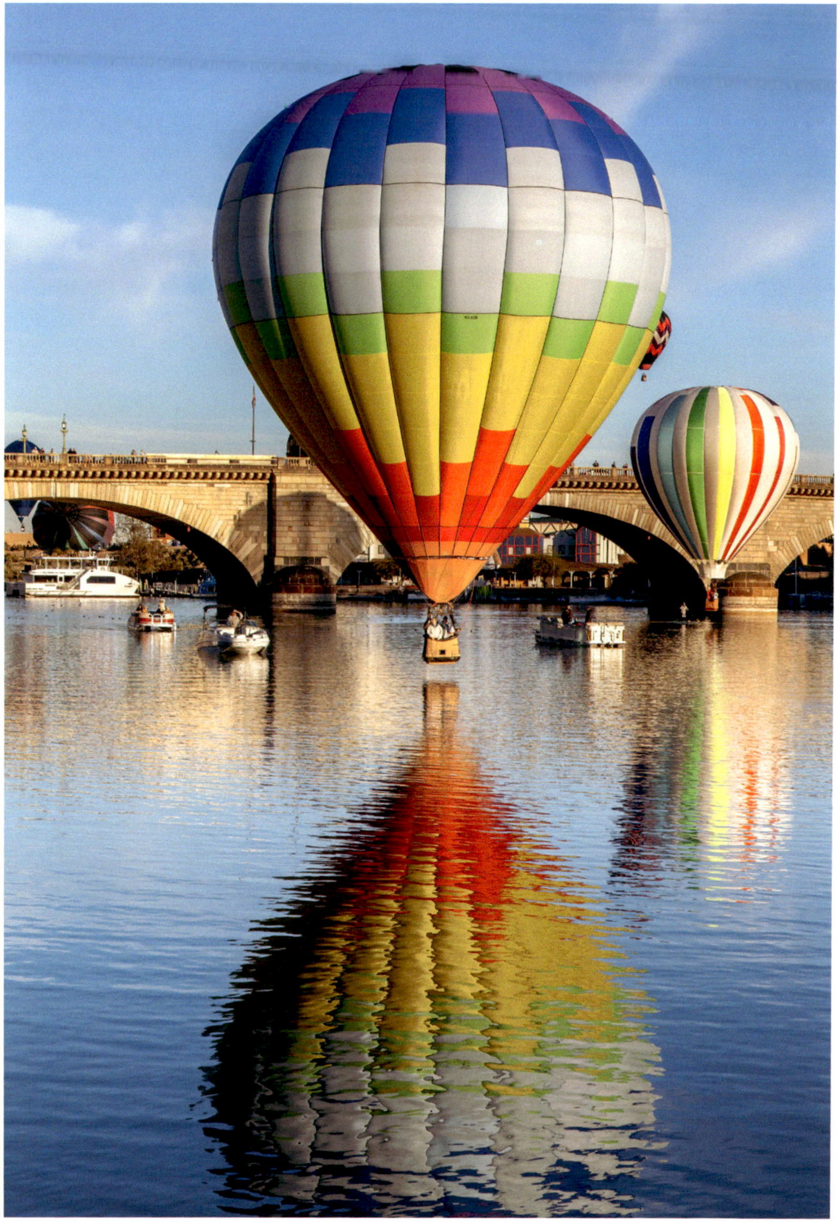

Left and below: At the Havasu Balloon Festival in Lake Havasu City, balloonists skim the water near the reconstructed London Bridge. Festival visitors get unique photos from inside a partially-inflated balloon open to the public. LARRY LINDAHL

Far left: Mexican gold poppies speckle the hills of the Phoenix Sonoran Preserve as a hot air balloon floats by on an early February morning. JAKE CASE

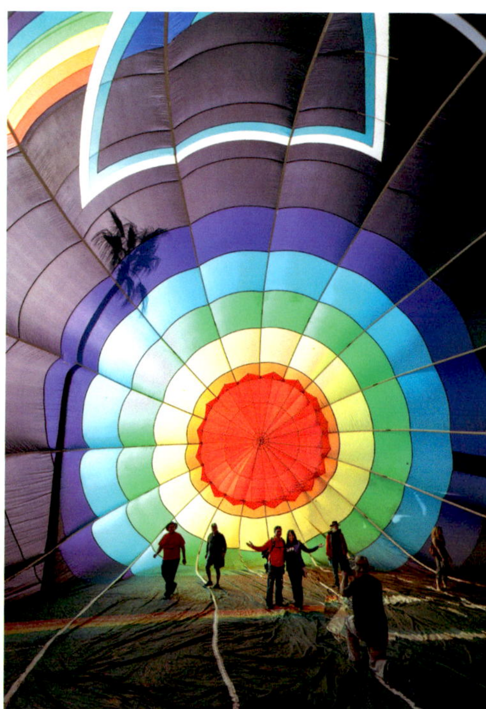

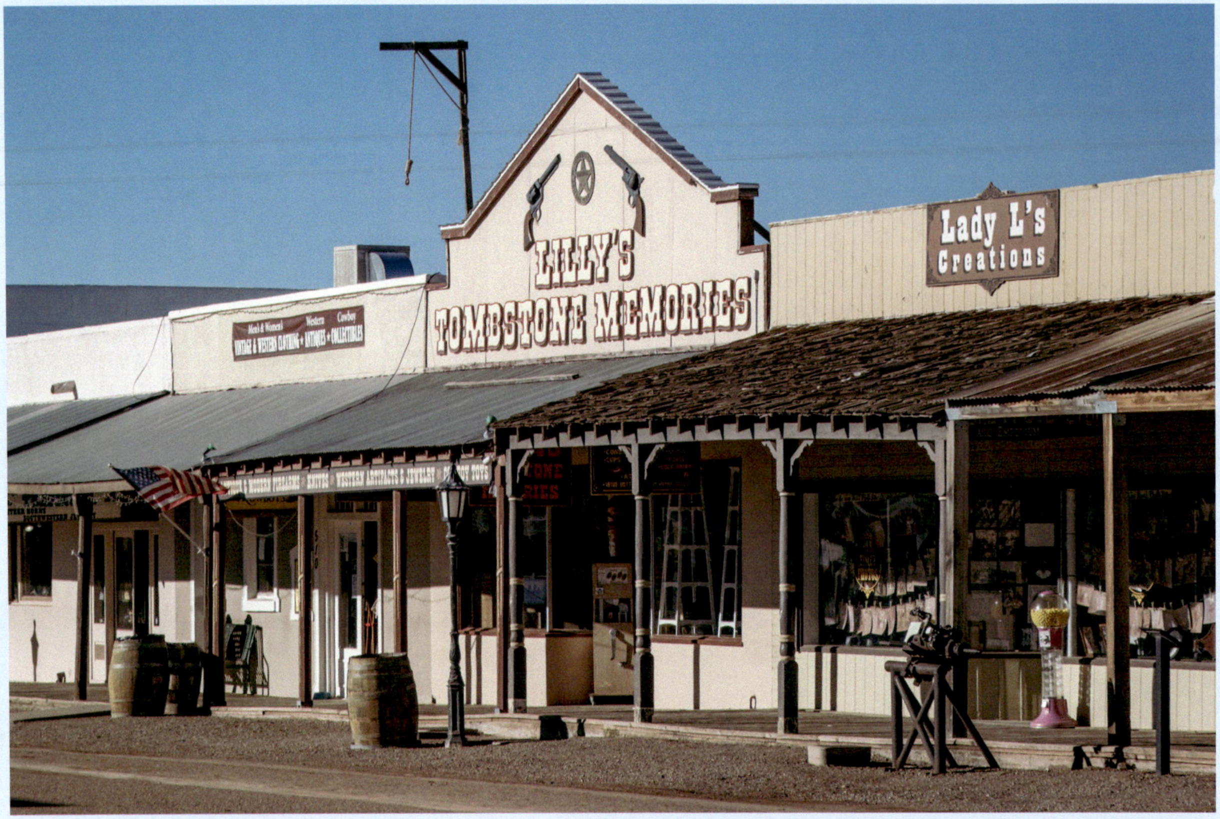

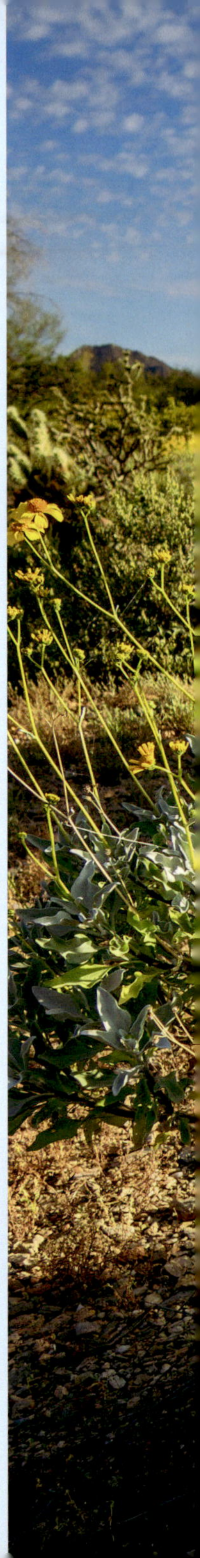

Above: Storefronts along Allen Street in historic Tombstone recall the spirit of the wild west that defines "The Town Too Tough To Die." JAKE CASE

Right: Gunfight re-enactors stand watch in the middle of a dusty street, commemorating the infamous battle at the O.K. Corral in Tombstone. JAKE CASE

Far right: Golden hedgehog cacti flank a fishhook barrel cactus and bloom in unison with yellow brittlebush on the footsteps of the McDowell Mountains. JAKE CASE

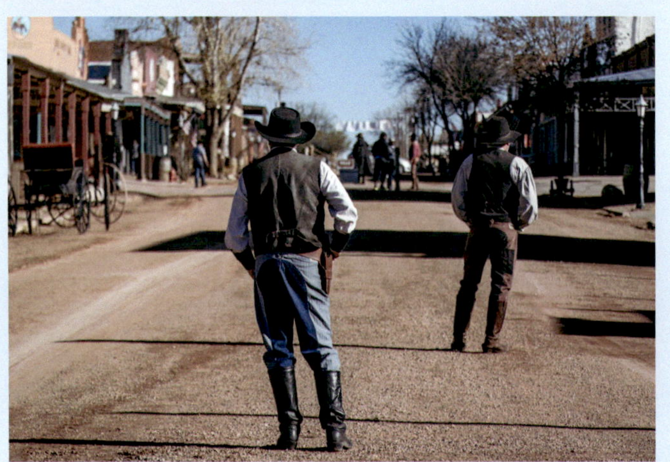

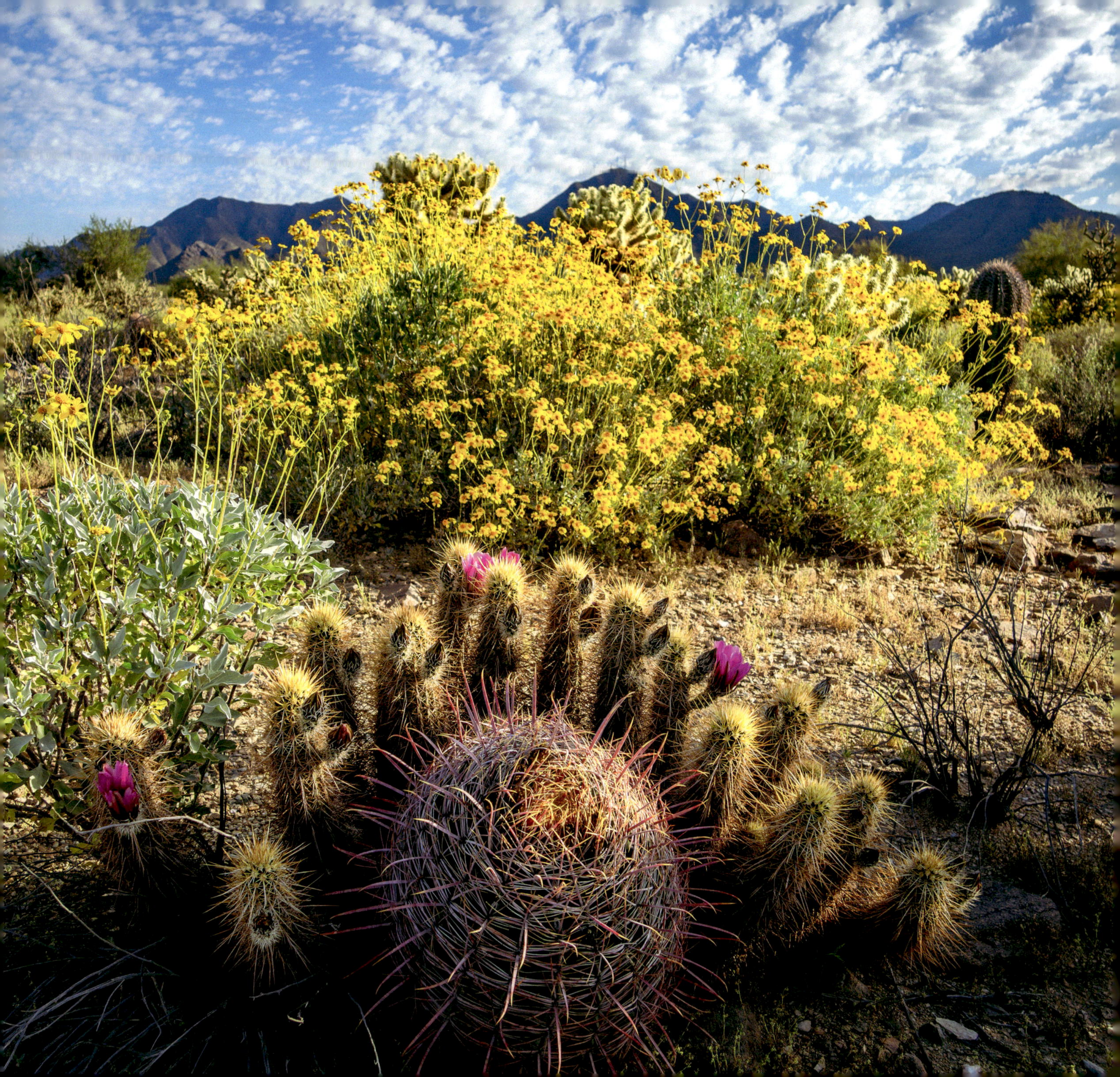

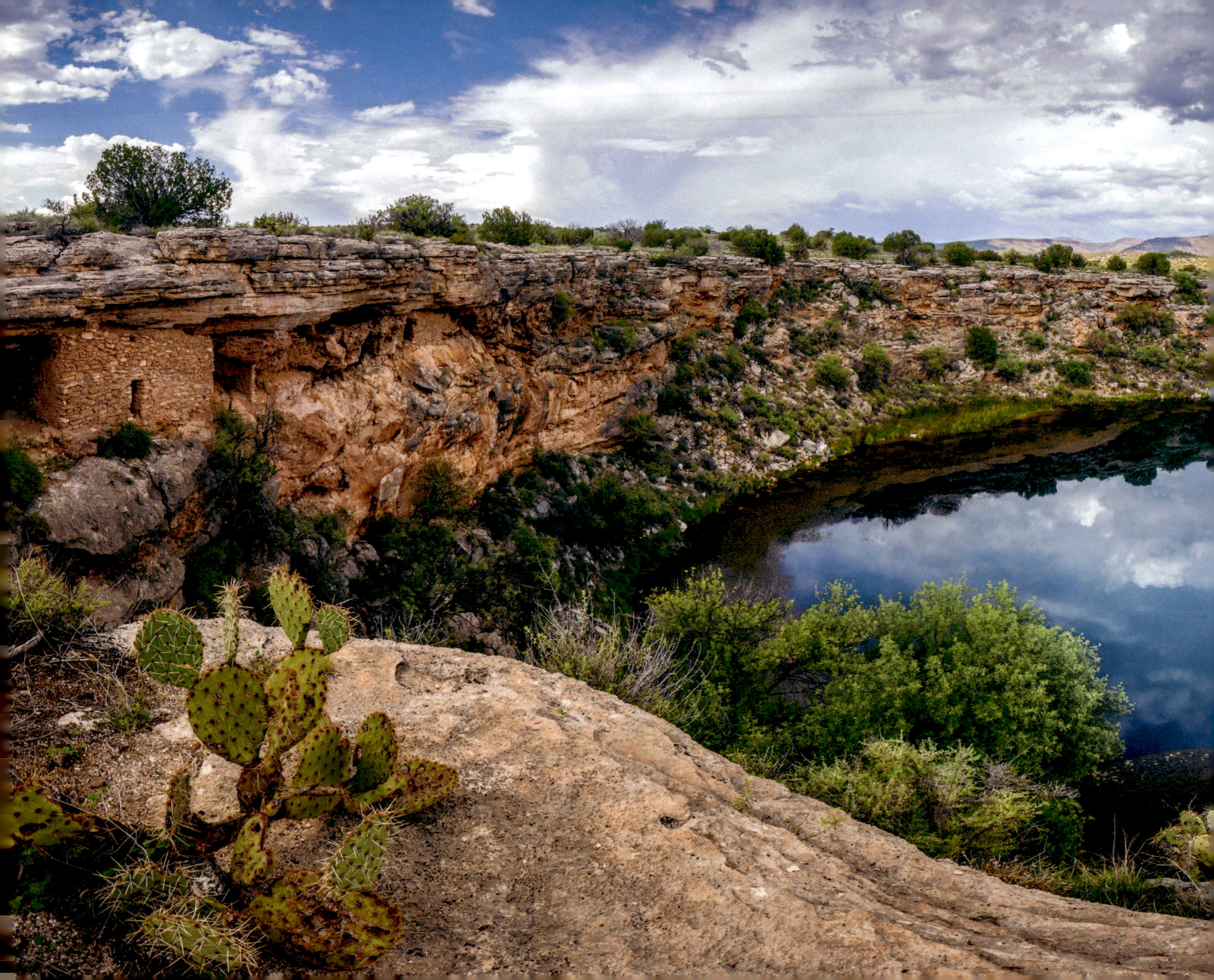

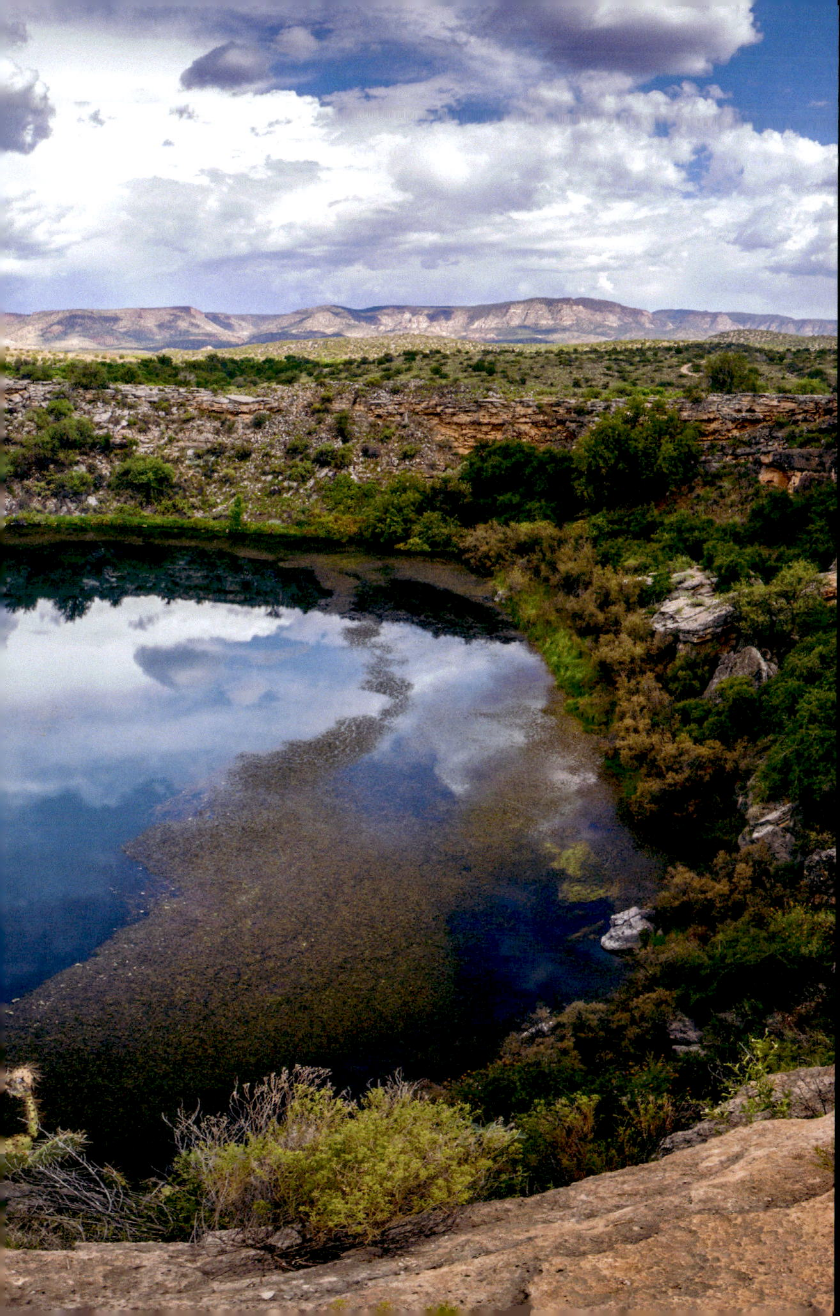

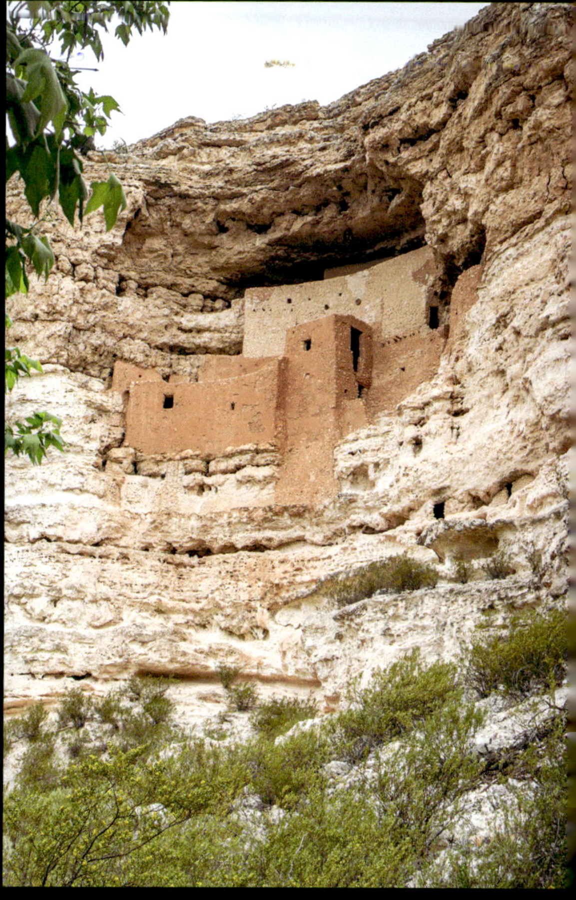

Above: Sinagua cliff dwellings built in the early 1100s stand stoically over the creosote bush and sycamore trees at Montezuma Castle National Monument. JAKE CASE

Left: Each day, Montezuma Well, a natural limestone sinkhole with a Sinagua-culture structure, is replenished with 1.5 million gallons of water from an underground spring. The site is a sub-unit of Montezuma Castle National Monument. LARRY LINDAHL

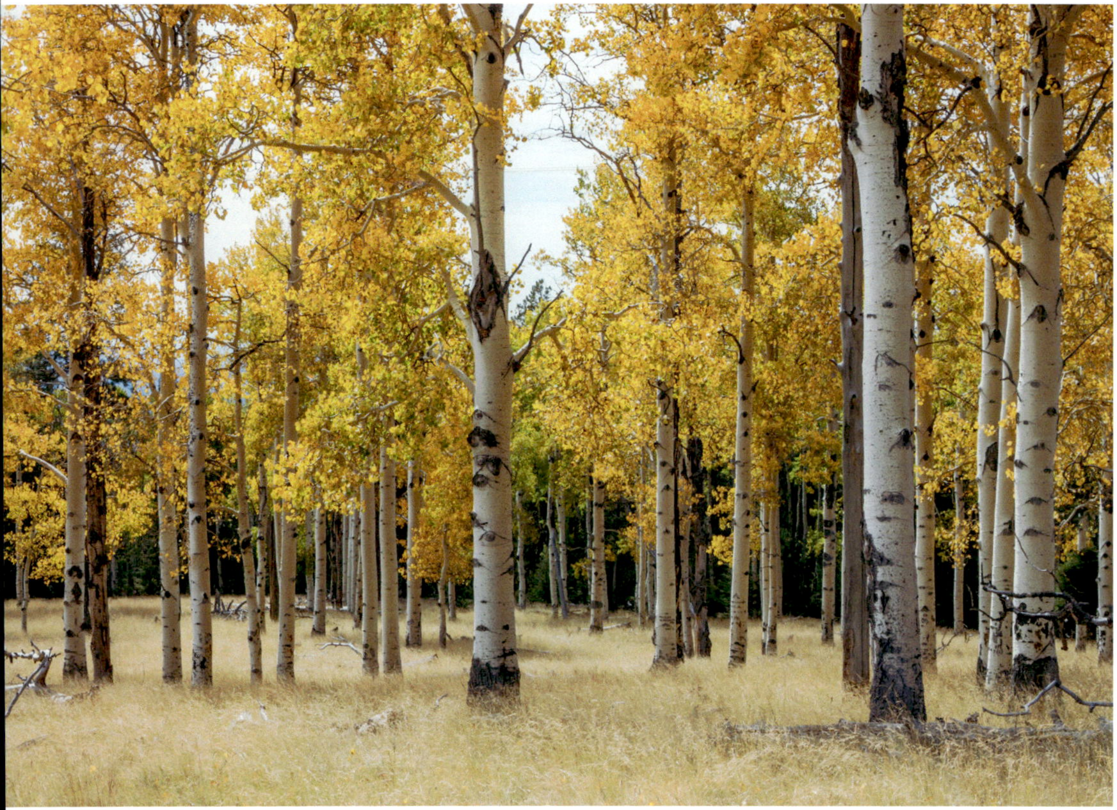

Above: Quaking aspen show their fall colors along the Kachina Trail on the southern slope of the San Francisco Peaks. JAKE CASE

Right: Autumn leaves freckle water-sculpted basalt boulders. JAKE CASE

Far right: Autumn-gold aspen trees spill across the Inner Basin of the San Francisco Peaks, near Flagstaff. LARRY LINDAHL

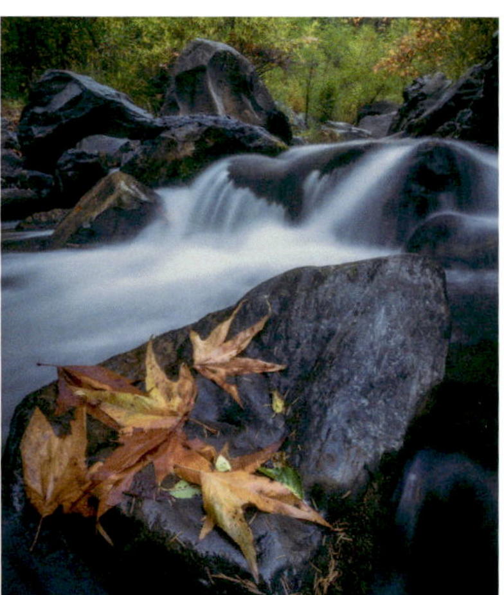

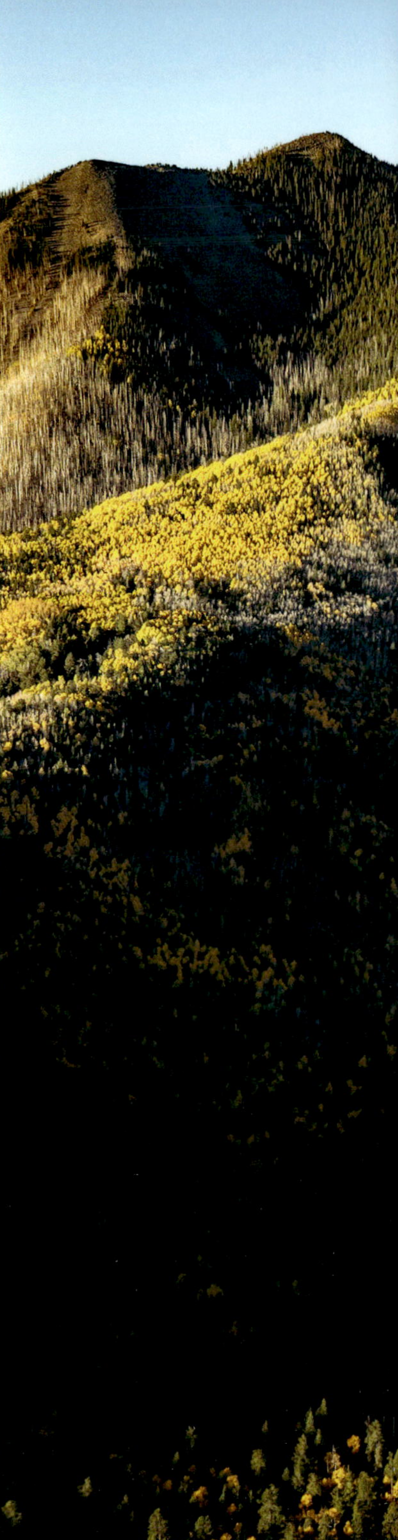

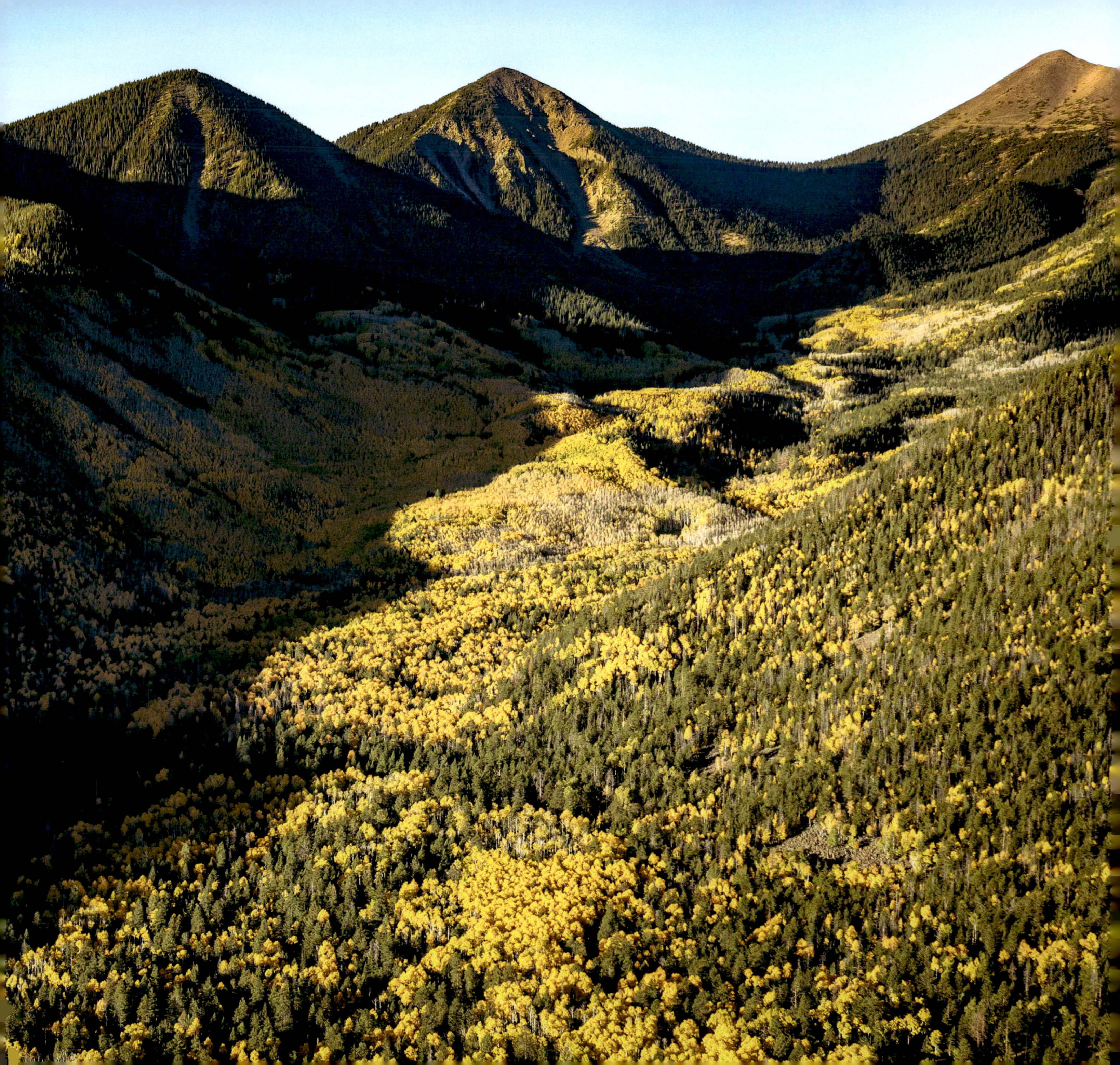

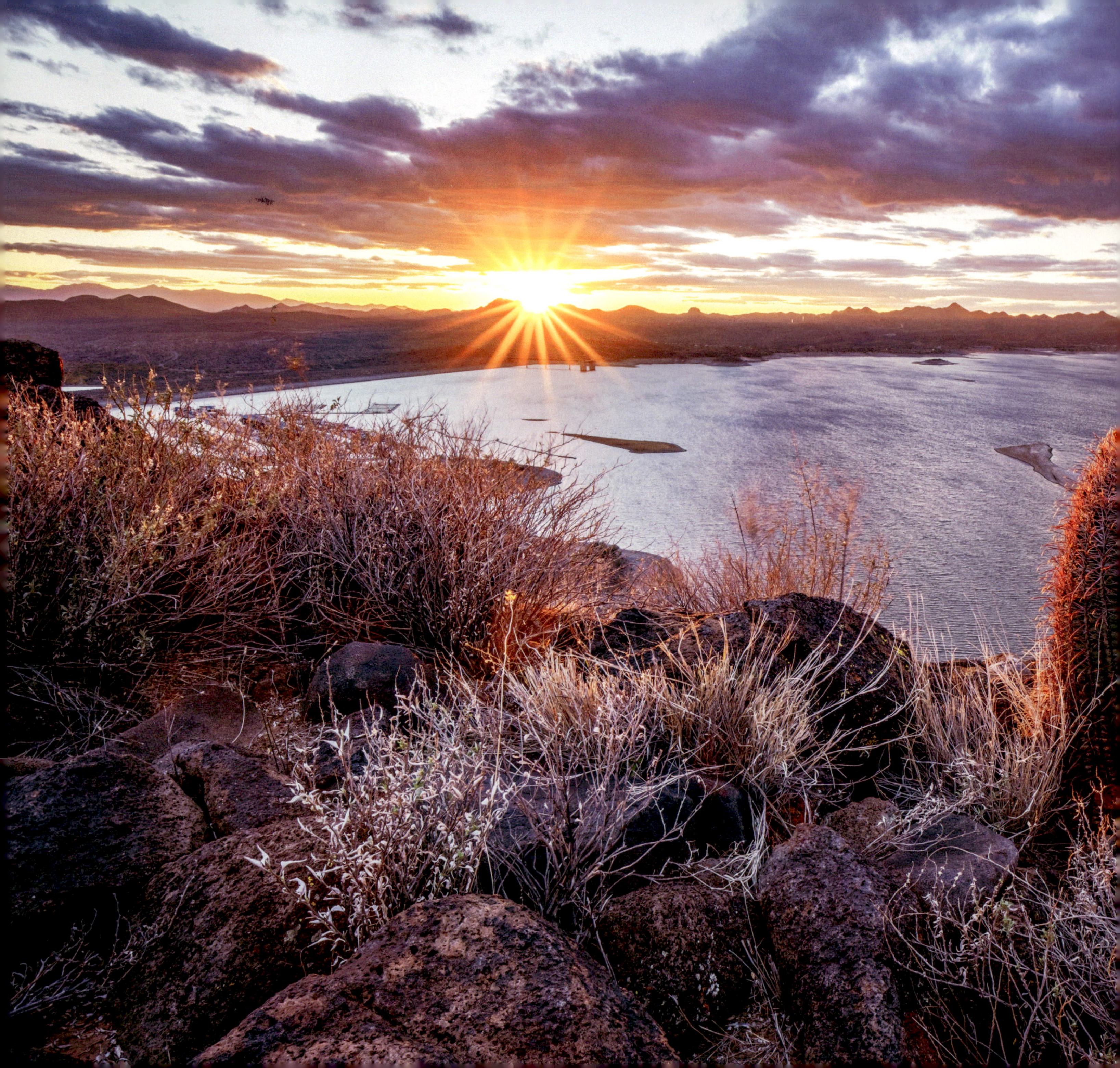

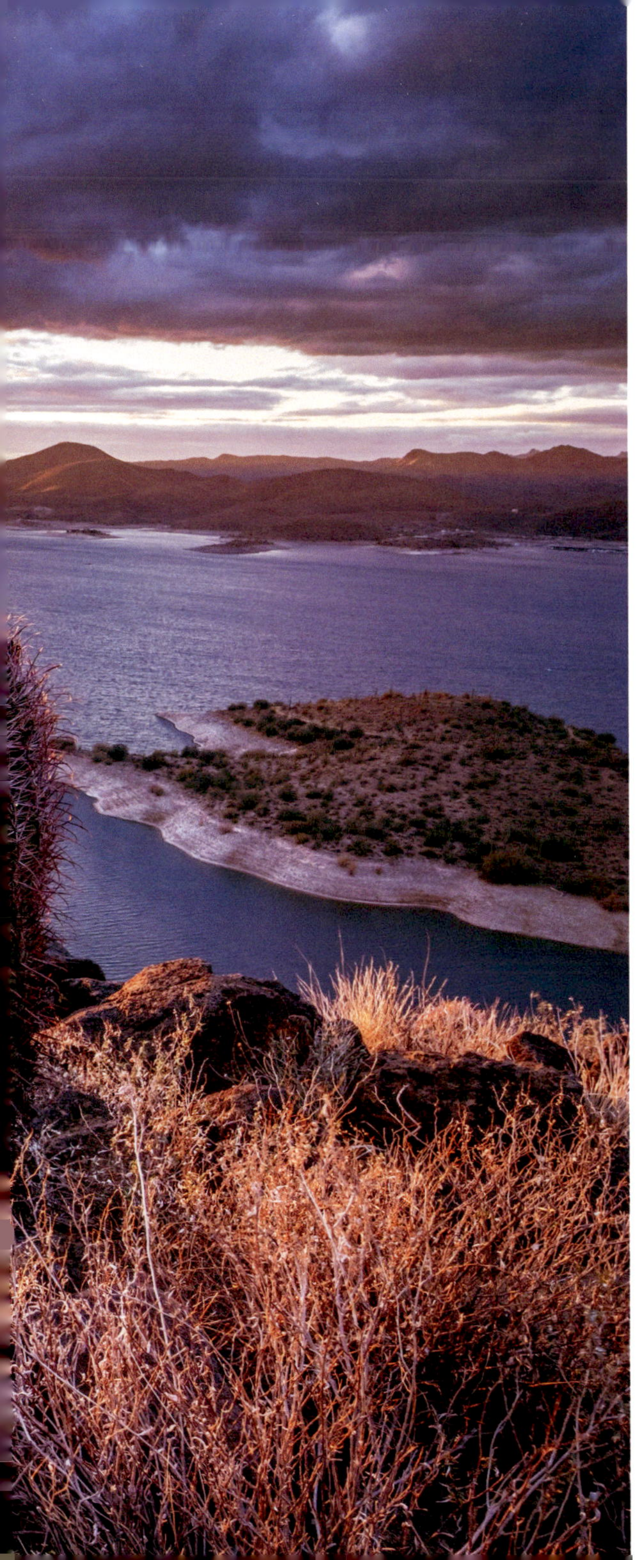

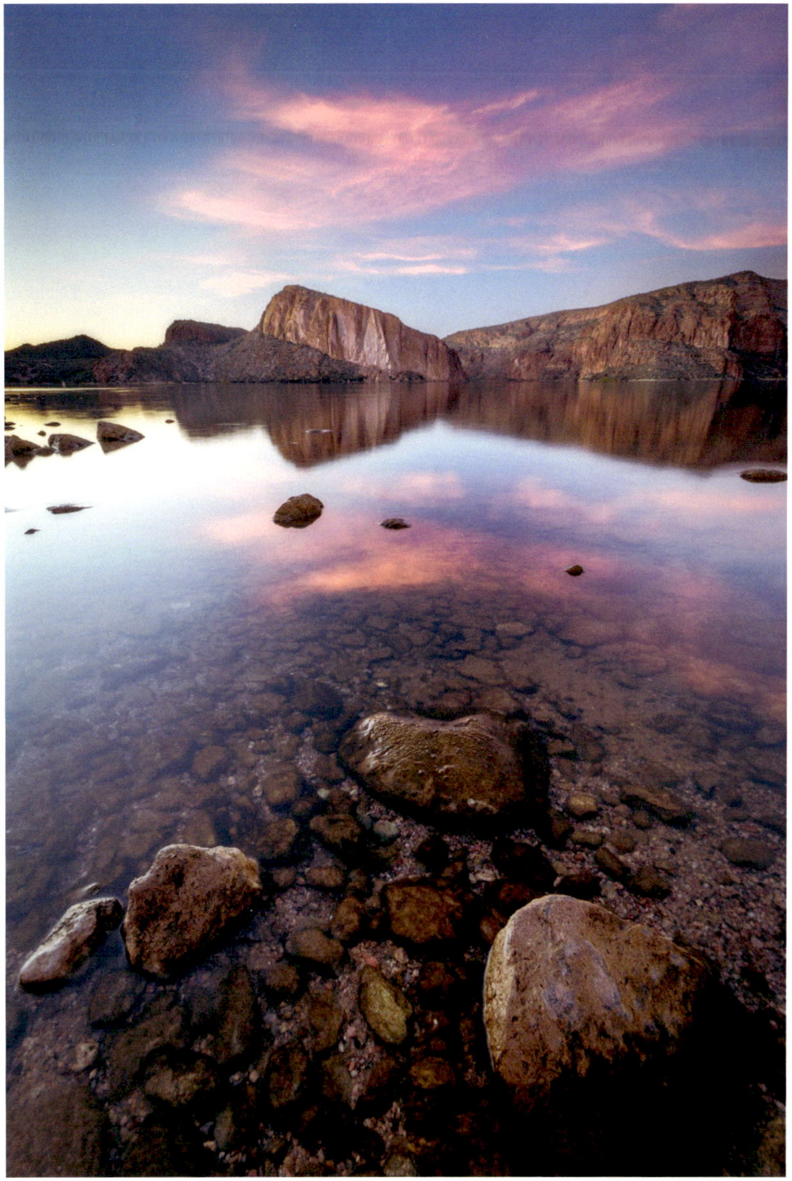

Above: Canyon Lake, one of four major reservoirs on the Salt River east of Phoenix, reflects the vibrant colors of a winter sunset. JAKE CASE

Left: A fishhook barrel cactus stands proudly at Vista Point, a rocky outcrop overlooking Lake Pleasant northwest of Phoenix. JAKE CASE

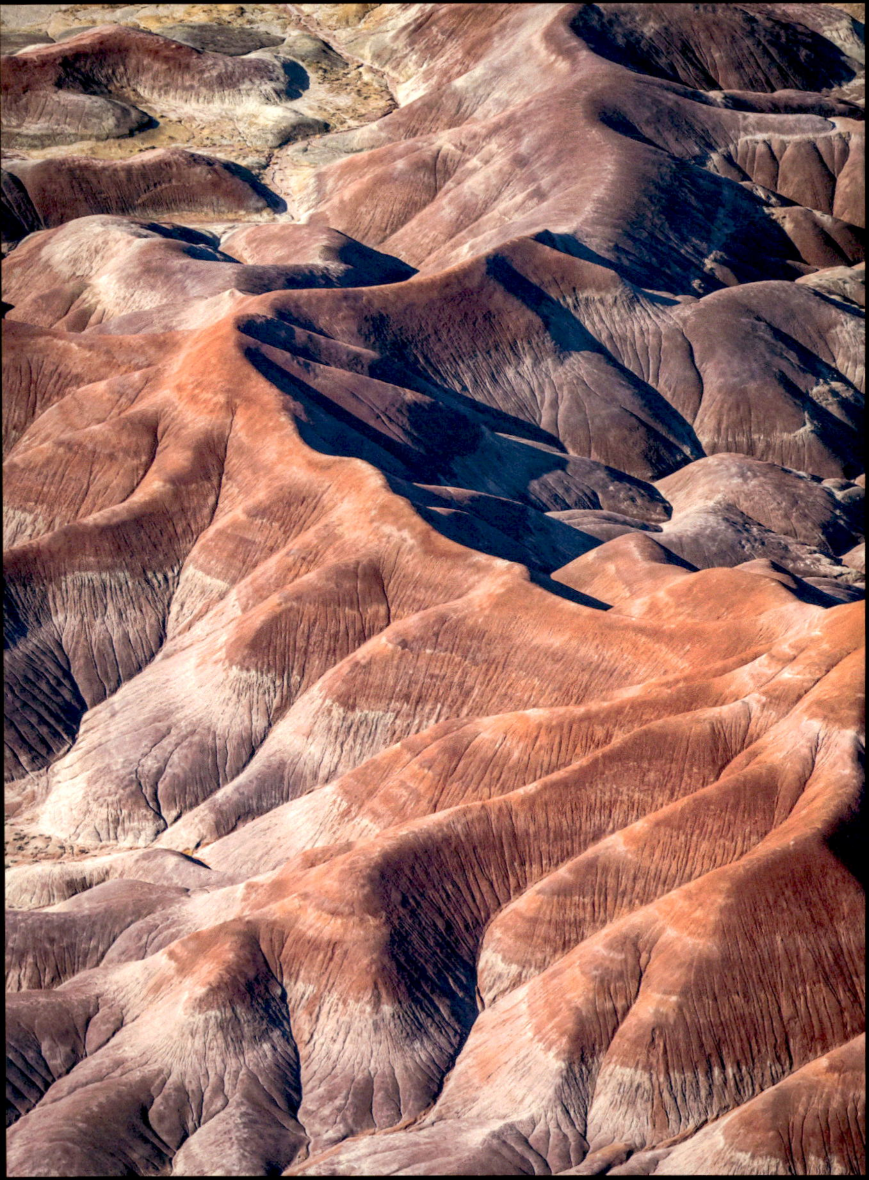

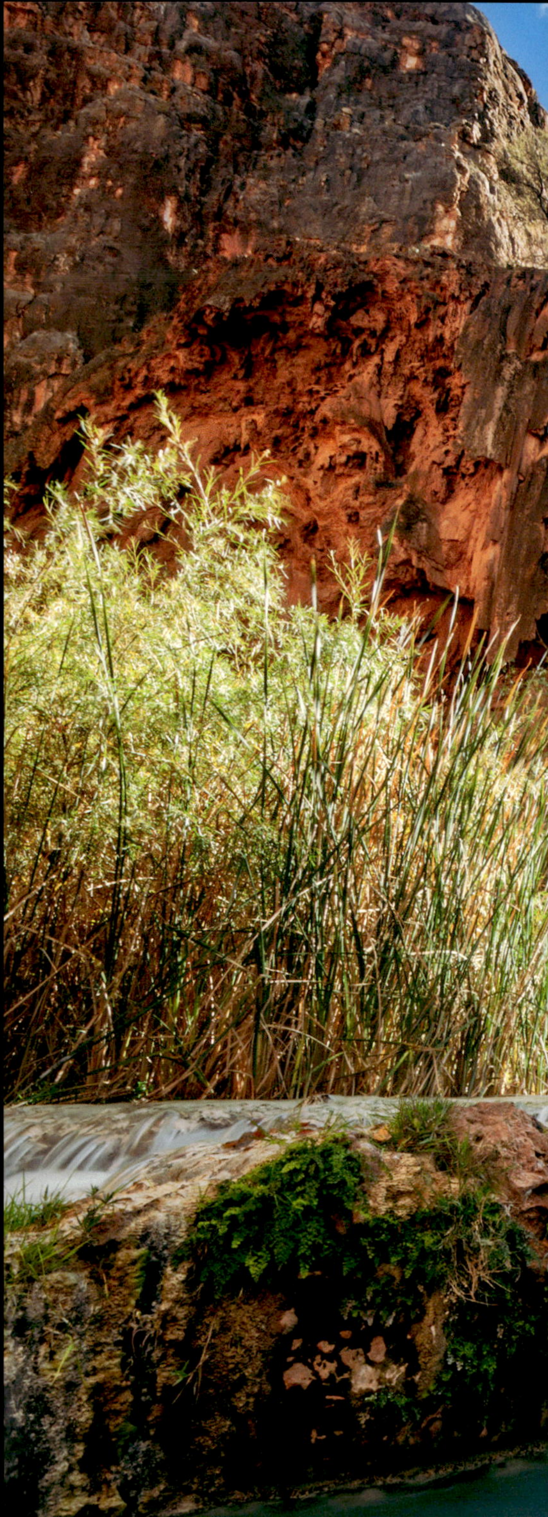

Above: The striated badlands ripple across the Painted Desert near Holbrook. LARRY LINDAHL

Right: Calcium carbonate-charged waters tumble over Havasu Falls, a 90-foot marvel on the Havasupai Reservation deep in the Grand Canyon. JAKE CASE

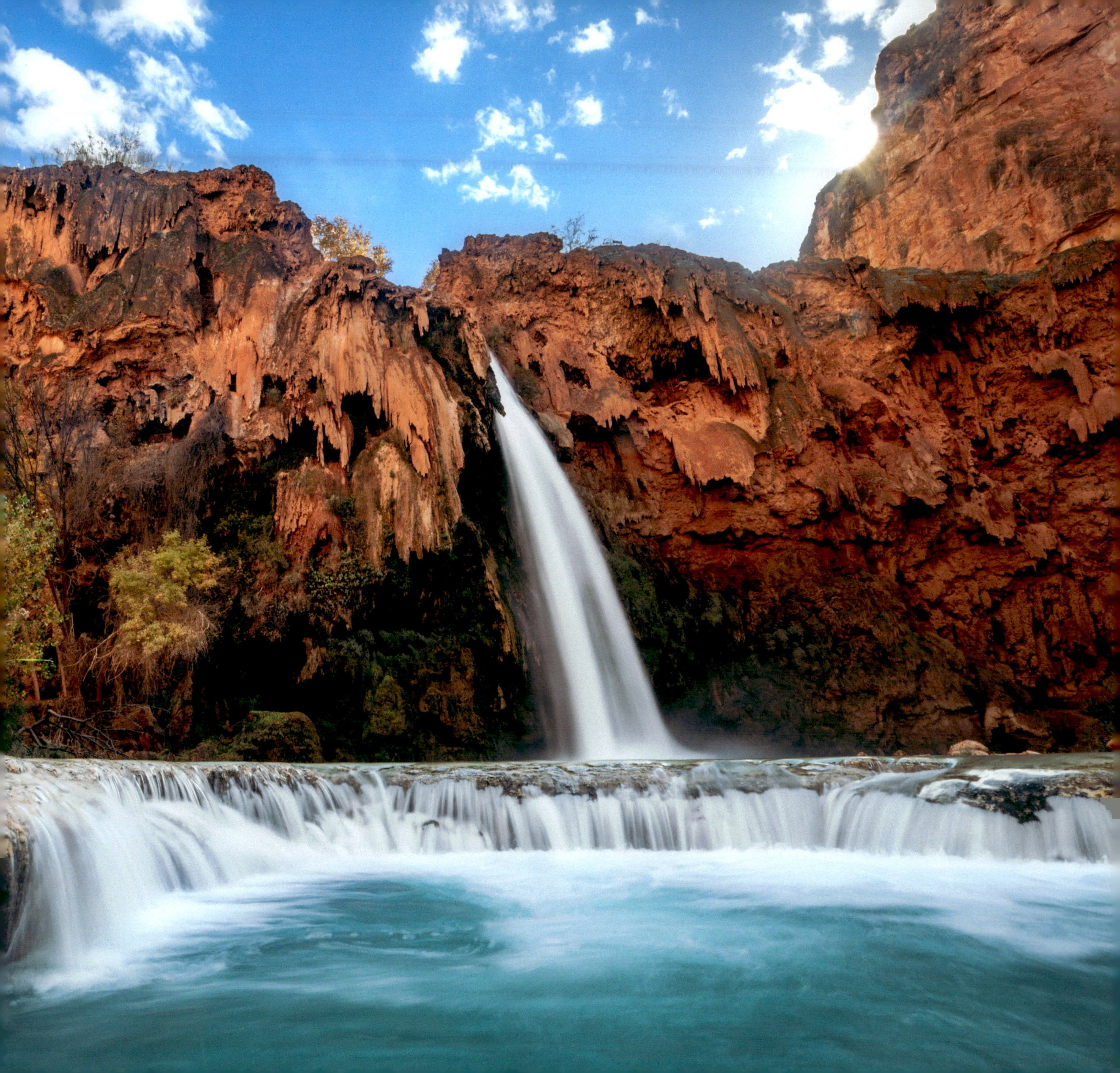

Right: The famous wooden cowboy welcomes visitors as they enter the arts district in the heart of Scottsdale. JAKE CASE

Far right: A sports car streaks through the roundabout around "Jack Knife," a sculpture commissioned by the City of Scottsdale and created by artist Ed Mell in 1993. JAKE CASE

Below: Geraniums offer a splash of color at Scottsdale's "Bronze Horse Fountain." Artist Bob Parks gifted the piece to the city in 1989. JAKE CASE

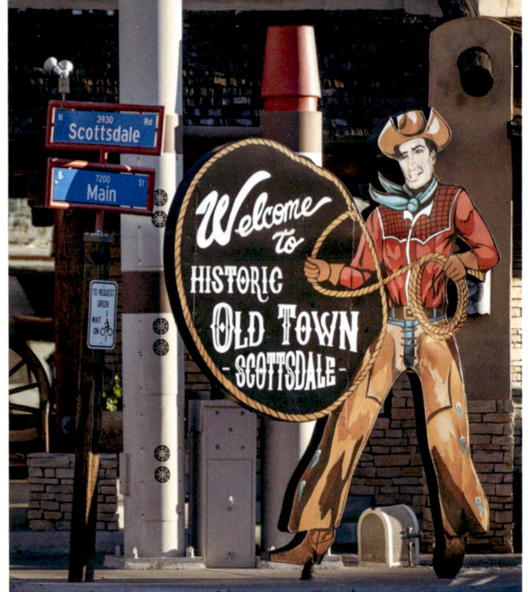

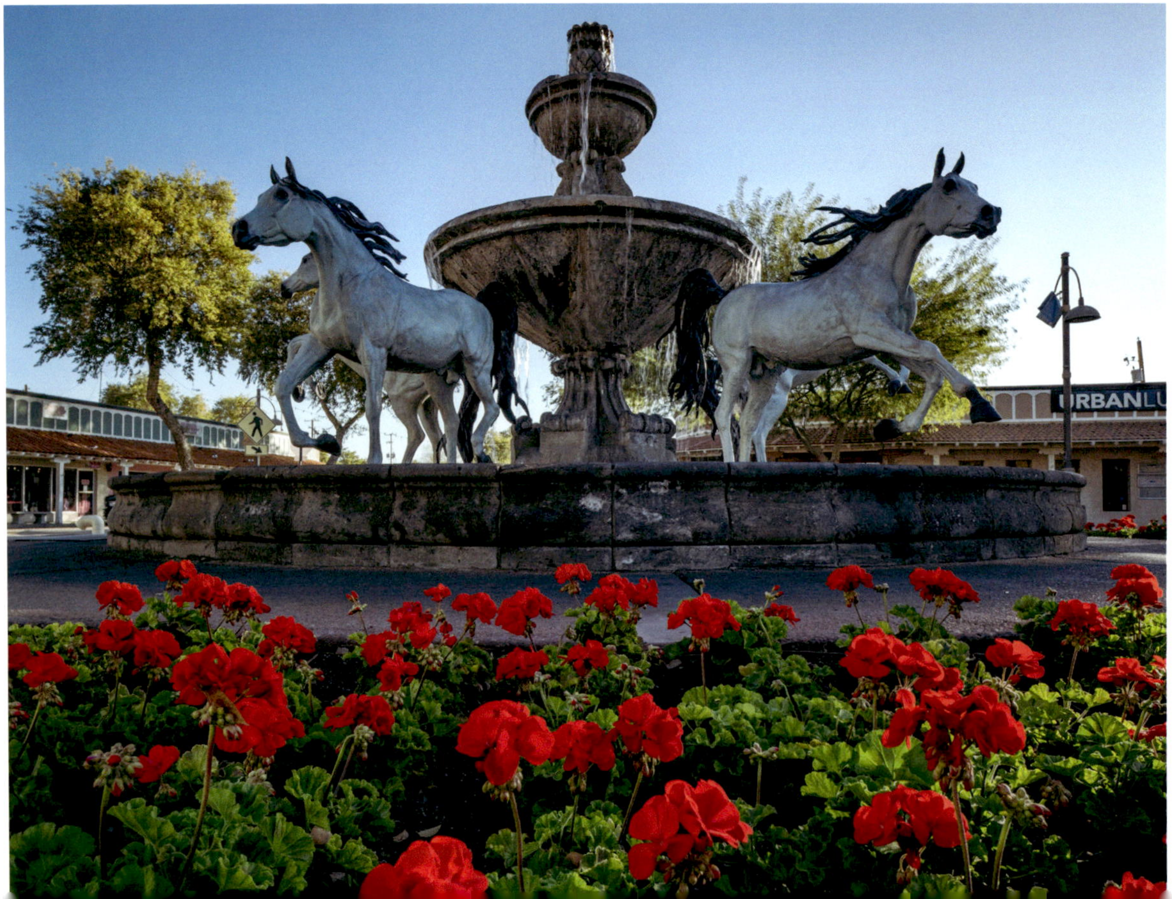

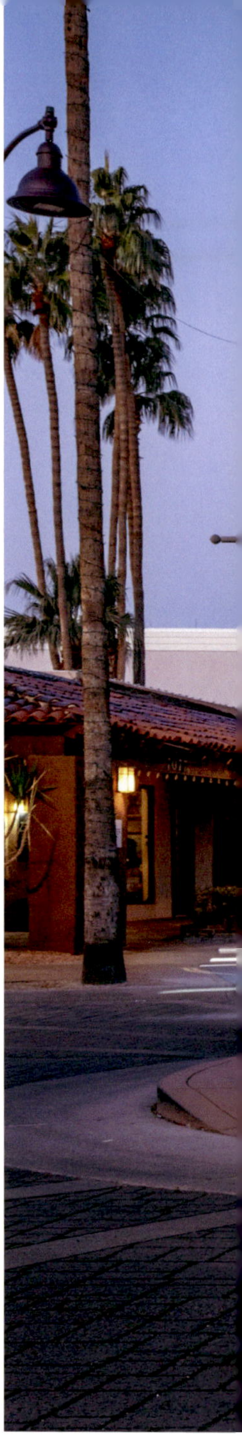

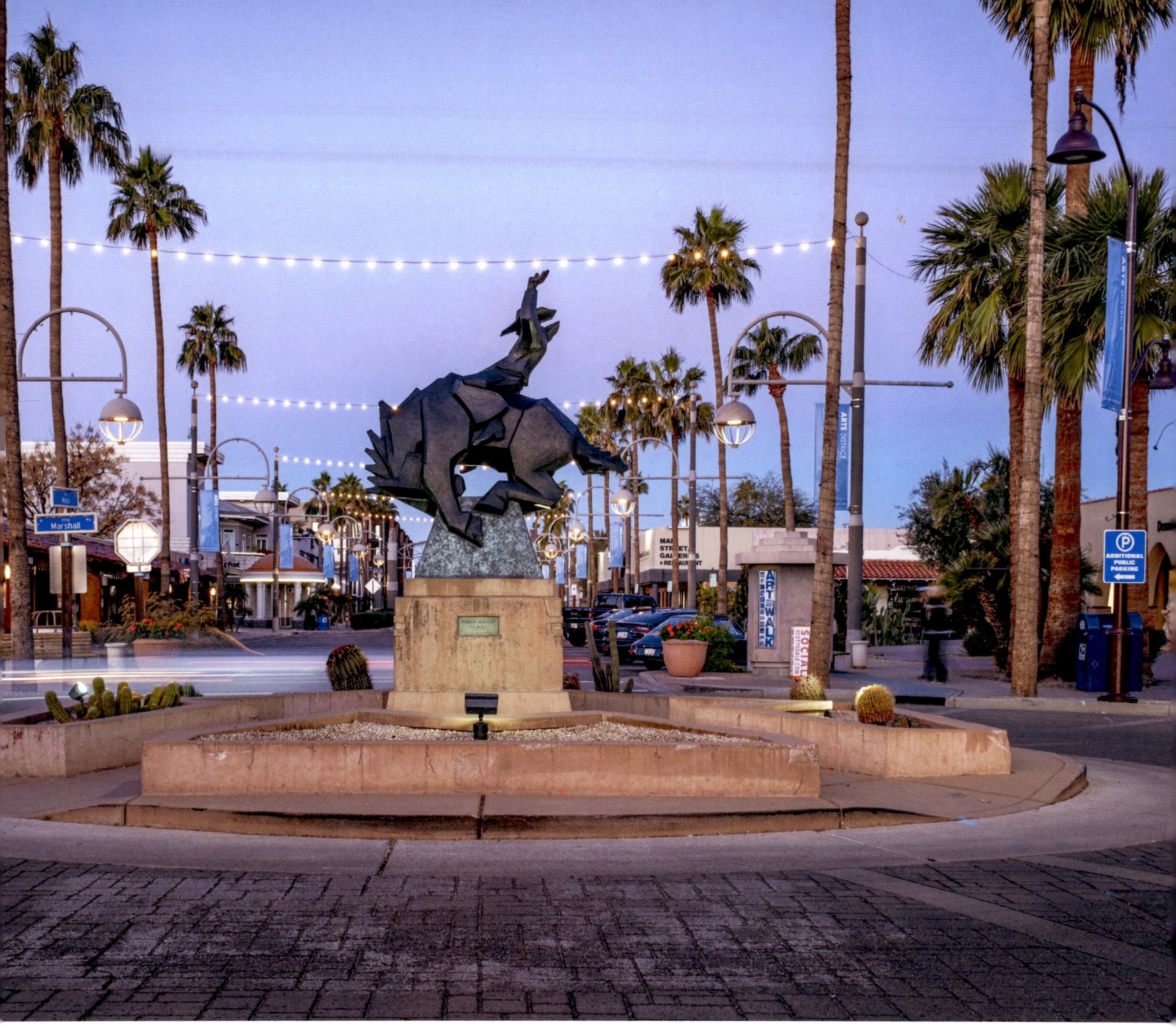
Marshall
ARTS DISTRICT
ART WALK
SOCIAL
SCOTTSDALE.COM
P
ADDITIONAL PUBLIC PARKING

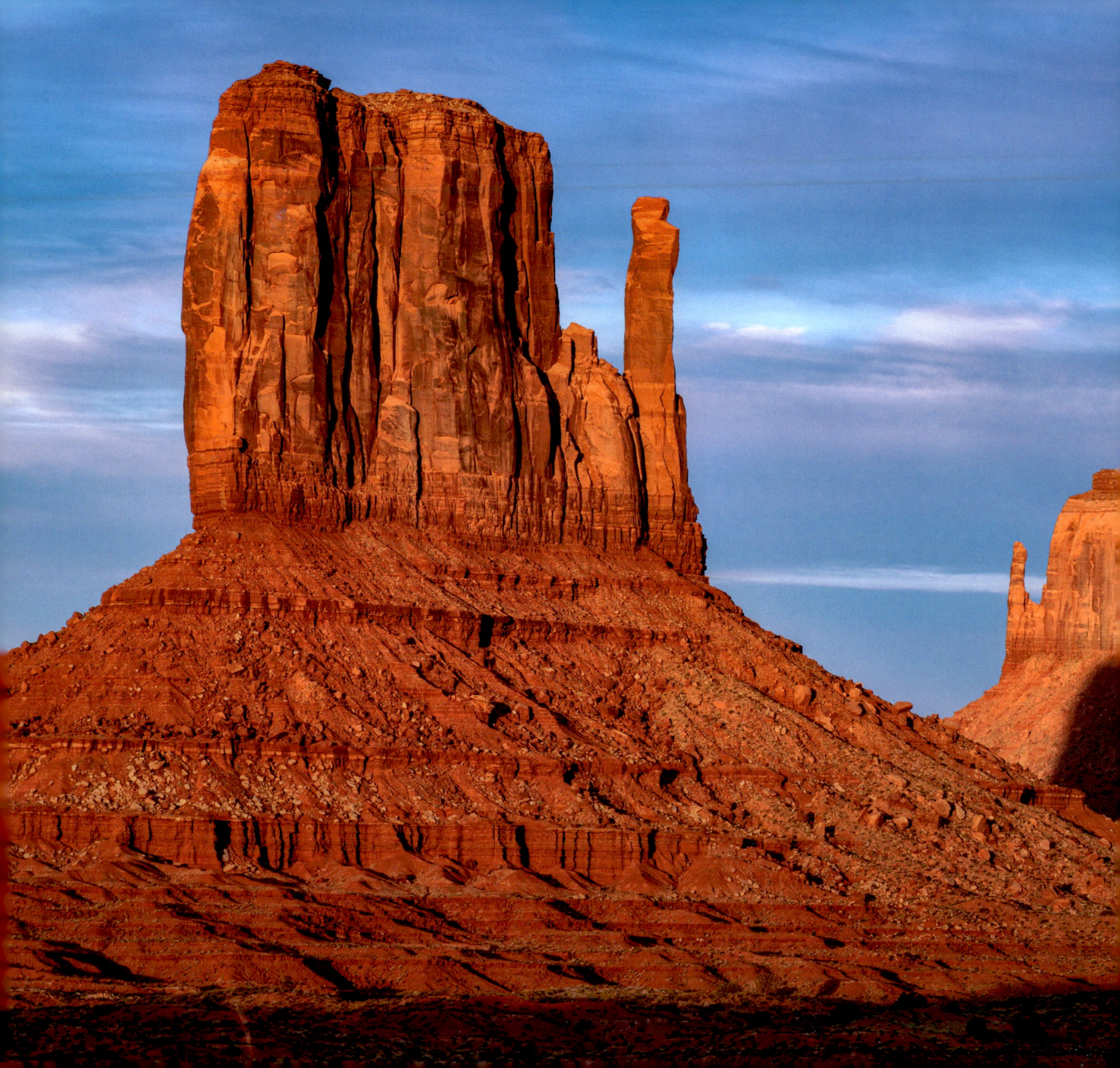

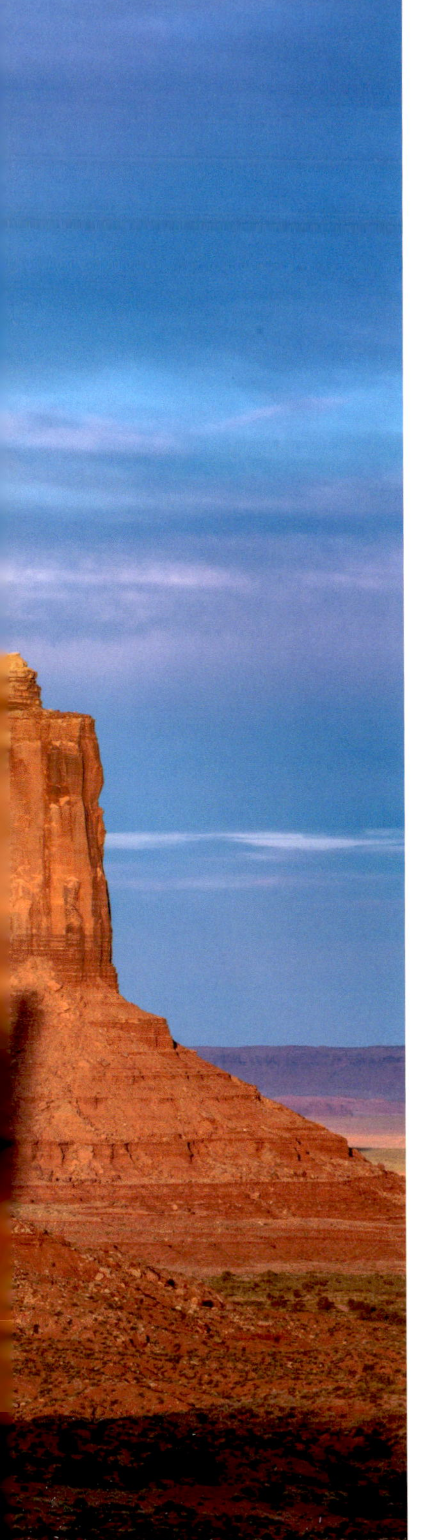

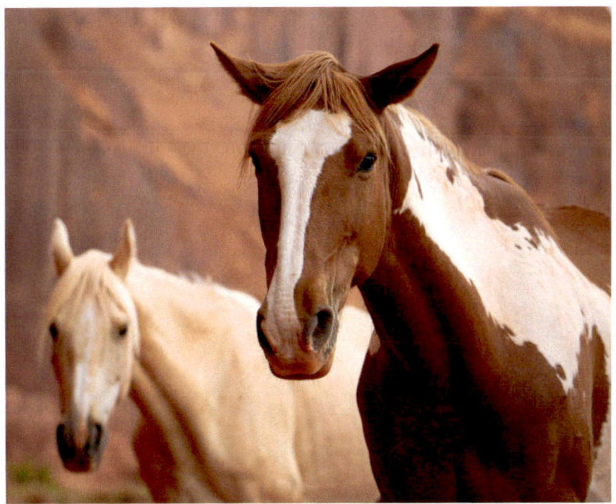

Left and below: Navajo lifeways continue with horses allowed to free roam and sheep herders tending their flocks from the saddle, as shown here in Monument Valley Navajo Tribal Park. LARRY LINDAHL

Far left: The Mittens soar more than 850 feet above the floor of Monument Valley. LARRY LINDAHL

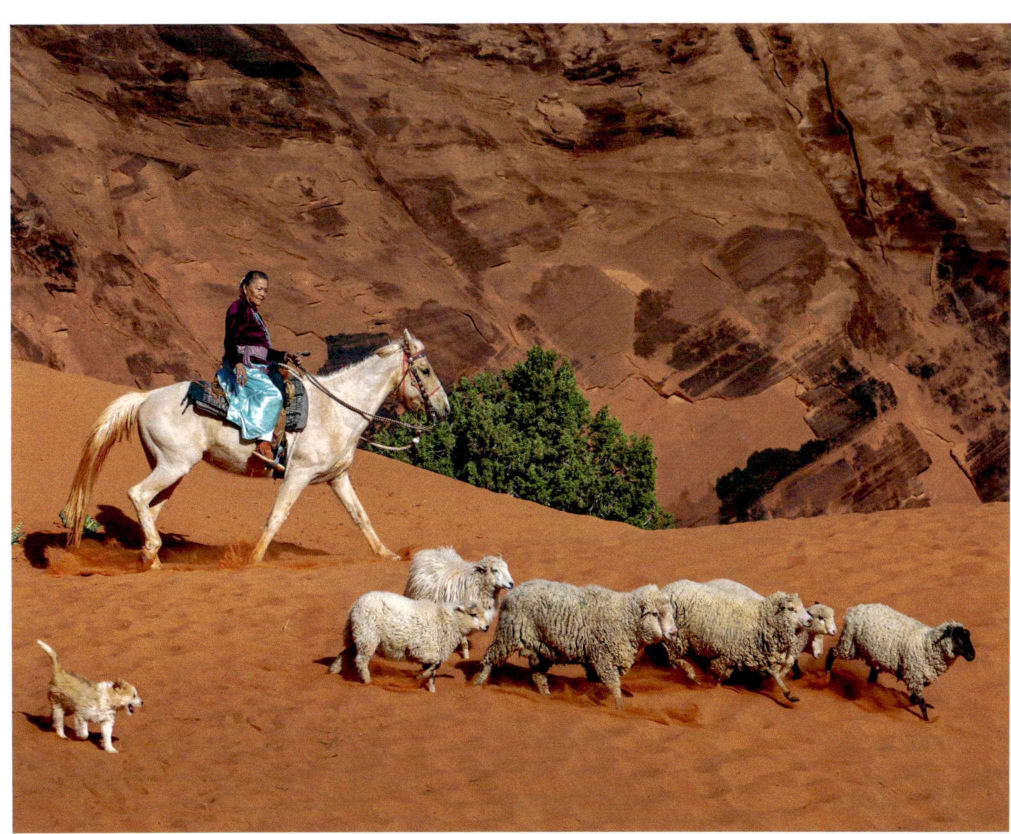

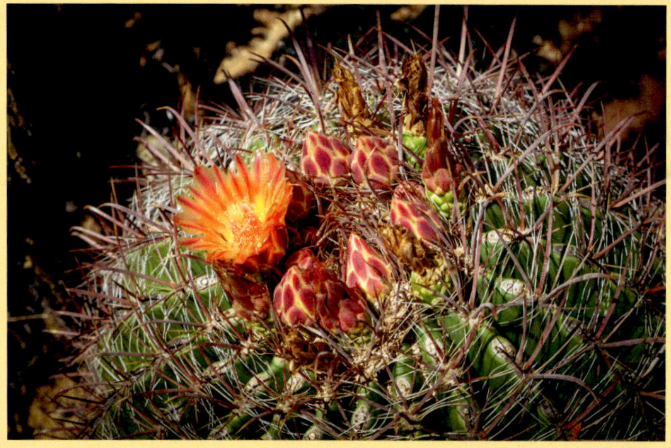

Above: Buds begin to open on a fishhook barrel cactus at the Arizona Sonoran Desert Museum in Tucson. LARRY LINDAHL

Right: The golden hues of dawn glow over downtown Tucson as viewed from Tumamoc Hill. JAKE CASE

Below: A cyclist takes advantage of a bike lane along Historic Fourth Avenue in a trend-setting district that local eateries and merchants showcase as "the Heartbeat of Tucson." LARRY LINDAHL

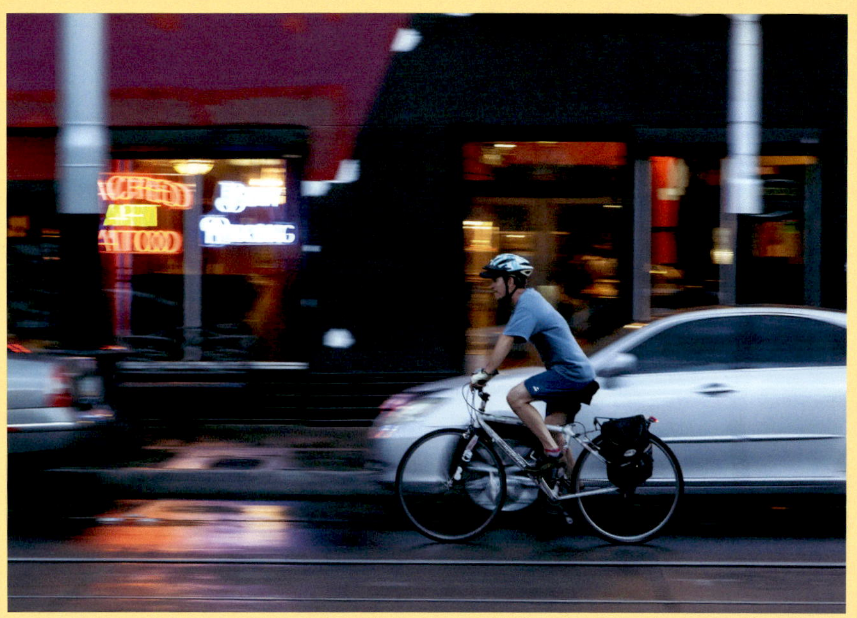

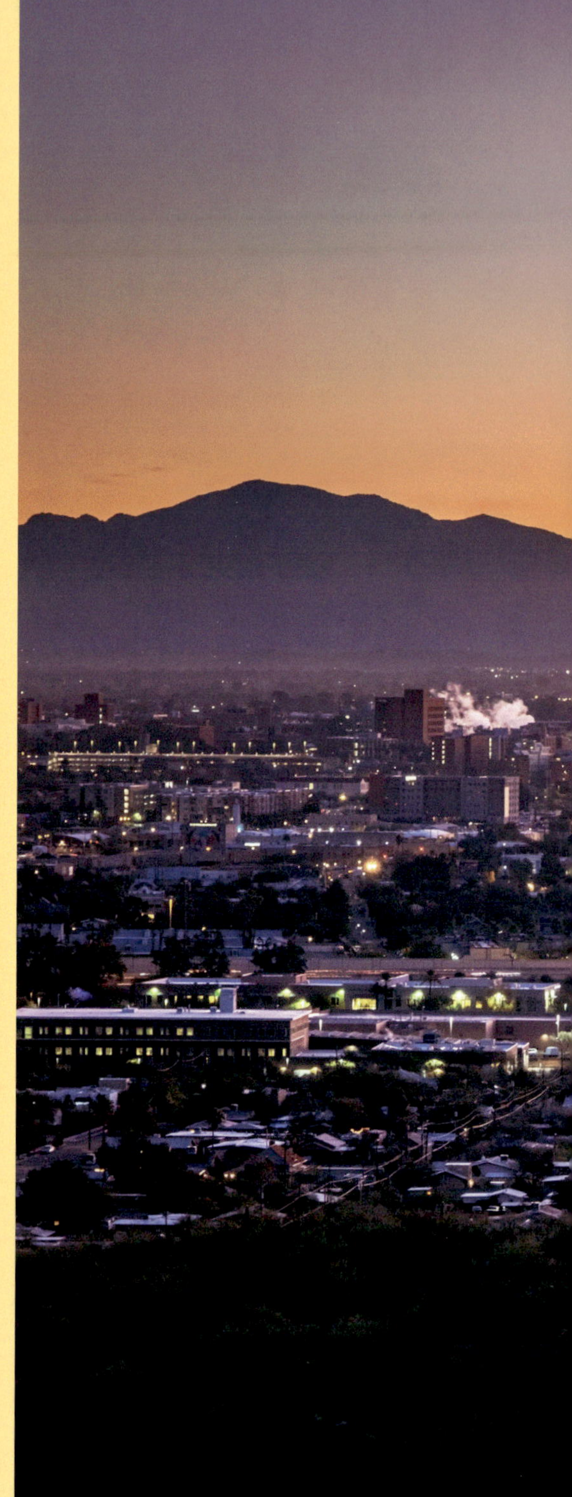

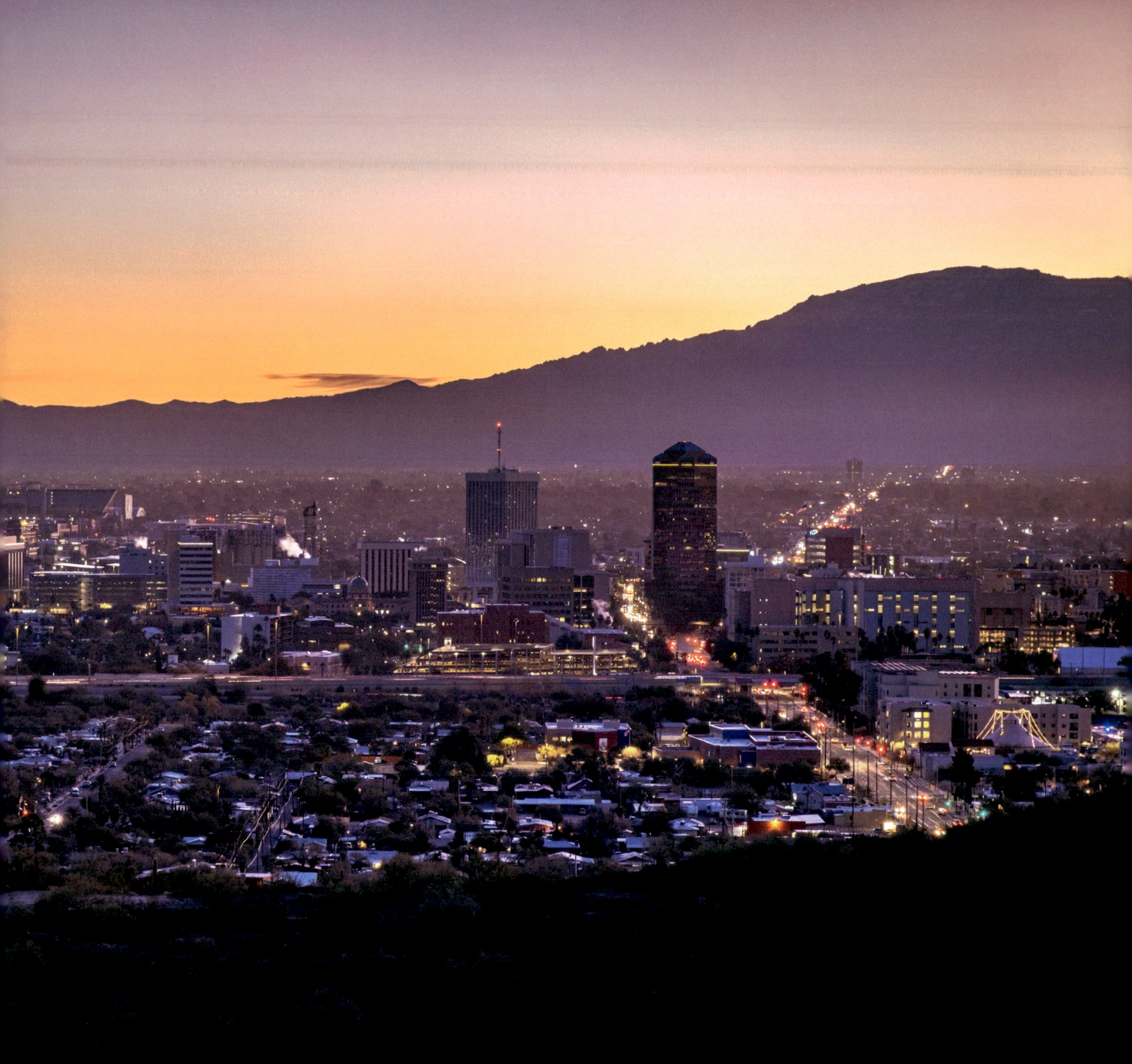

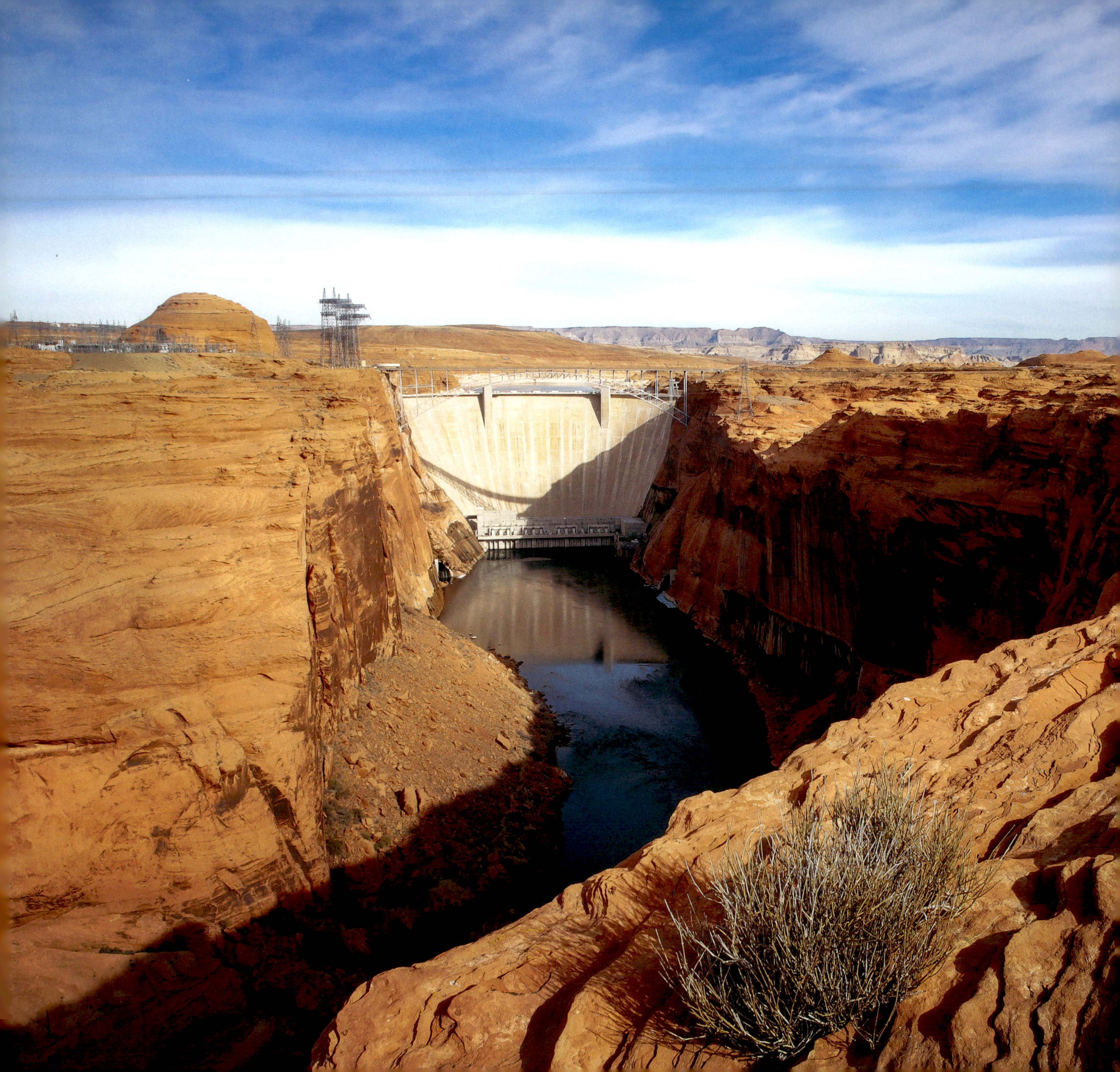

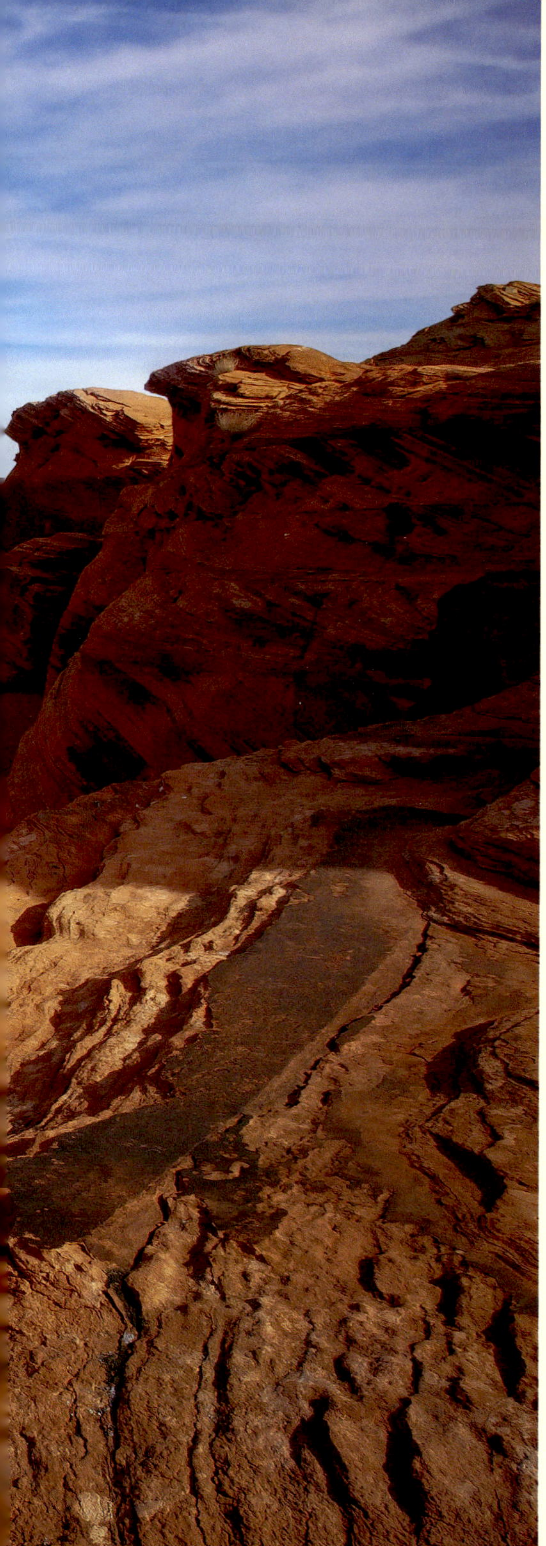

Left: Glen Canyon Dam impounds the Colorado River near Page, creating Lake Powell with 1,900 miles of shoreline. LARRY LINDAHL

Below: Soaring 726 feet above the Colorado River, Hoover Dam holds back Lake Mead. Downstream from the dam, the Black Canyon of the Colorado is popular with boaters who paddle its clear, cold waters. LARRY LINDAHL

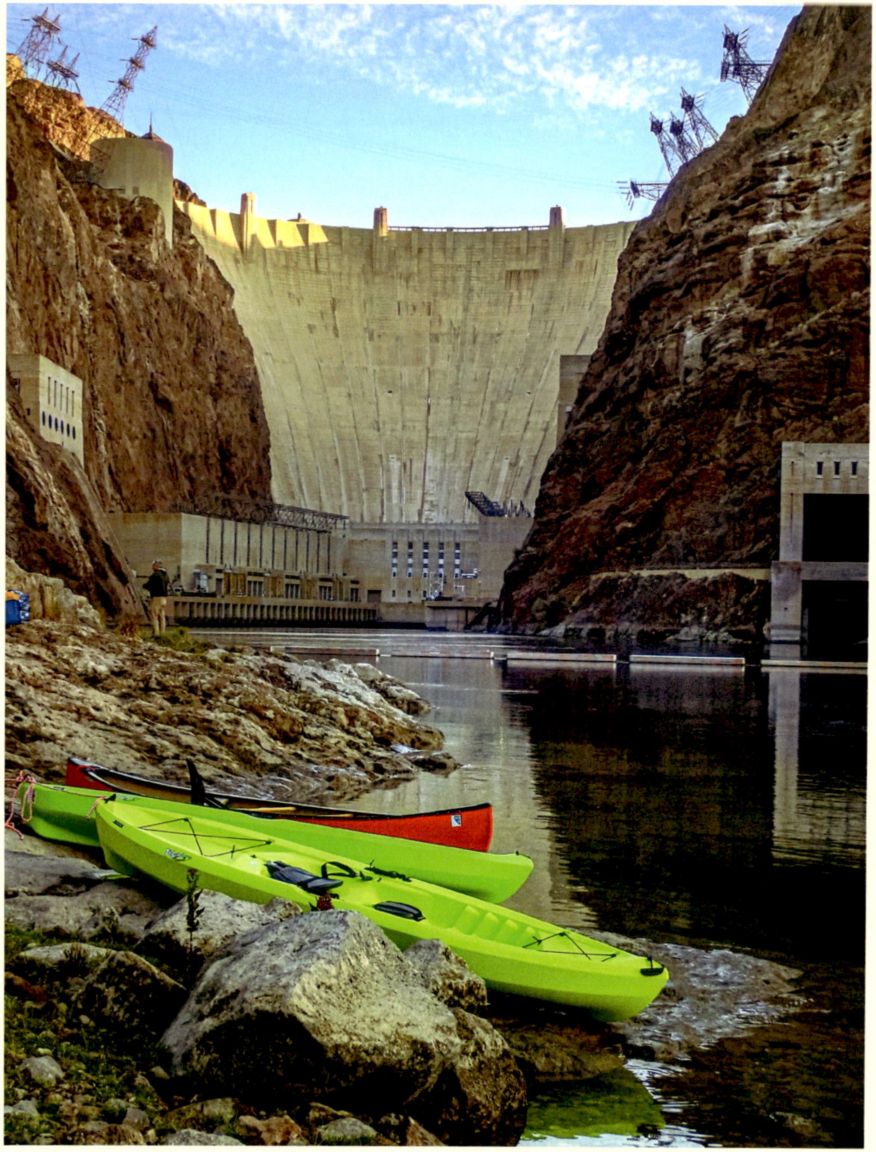

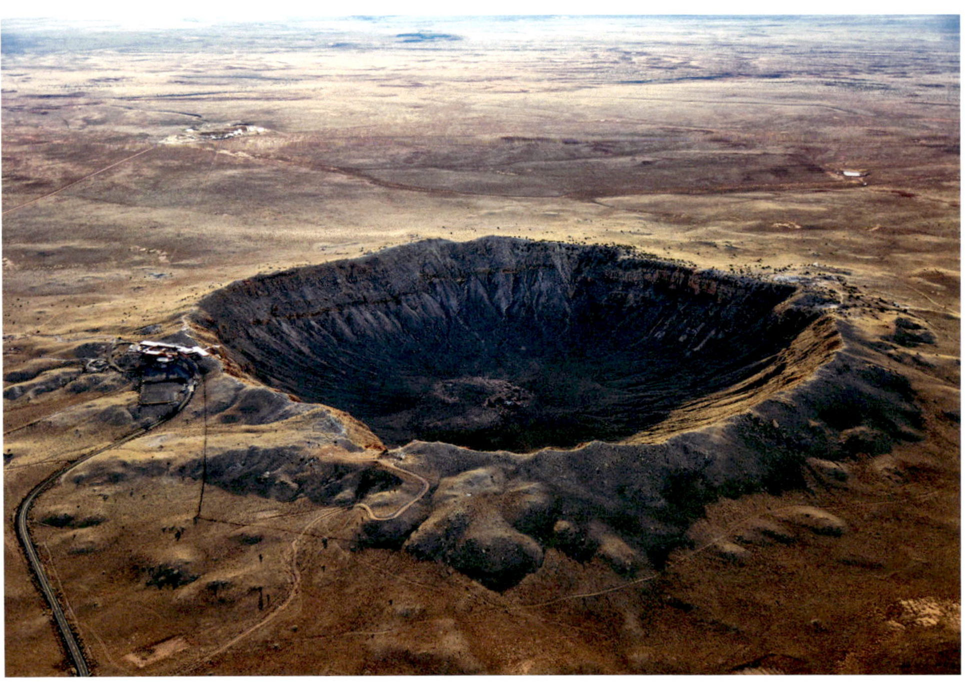

Above: About 50,000 years ago, a meteorite slammed into the ground east of present-day Flagstaff, leaving a divot three-quarters of a mile wide and 560 feet deep. Meteor Crater Natural Landmark offers guided rim tours and a gift and mineral shop. LARRY LINDAHL

Right: The deep red blossoms of the claretcup cactus give the plant its name. LARRY LINDAHL

Far right: Surrounding Lake Mead, the Mojave Desert is home to Joshua trees, banana yuccas, and other hardy and fascinating plants. LARRY LINDAHL

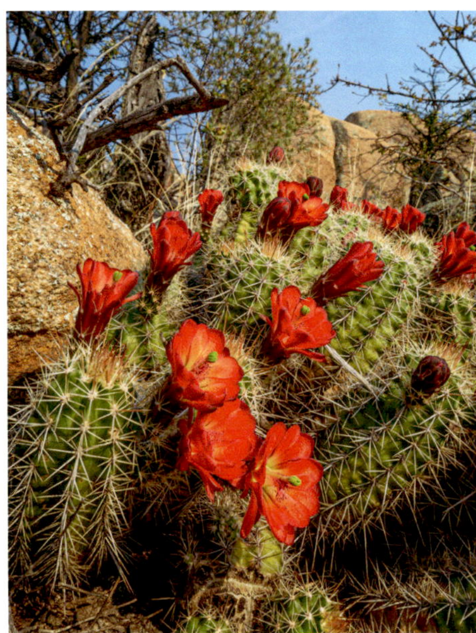

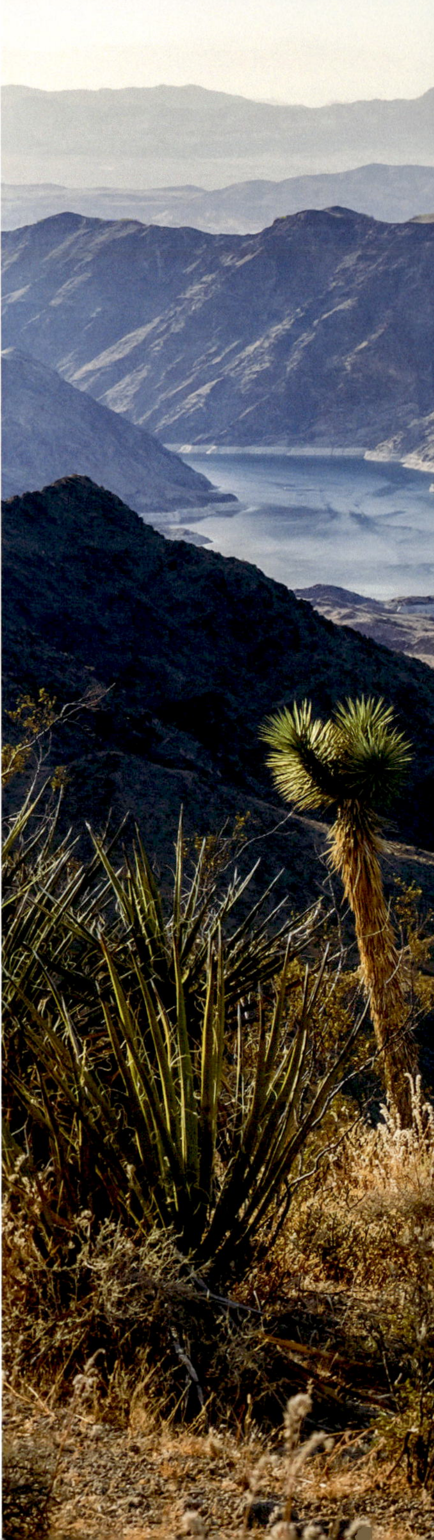

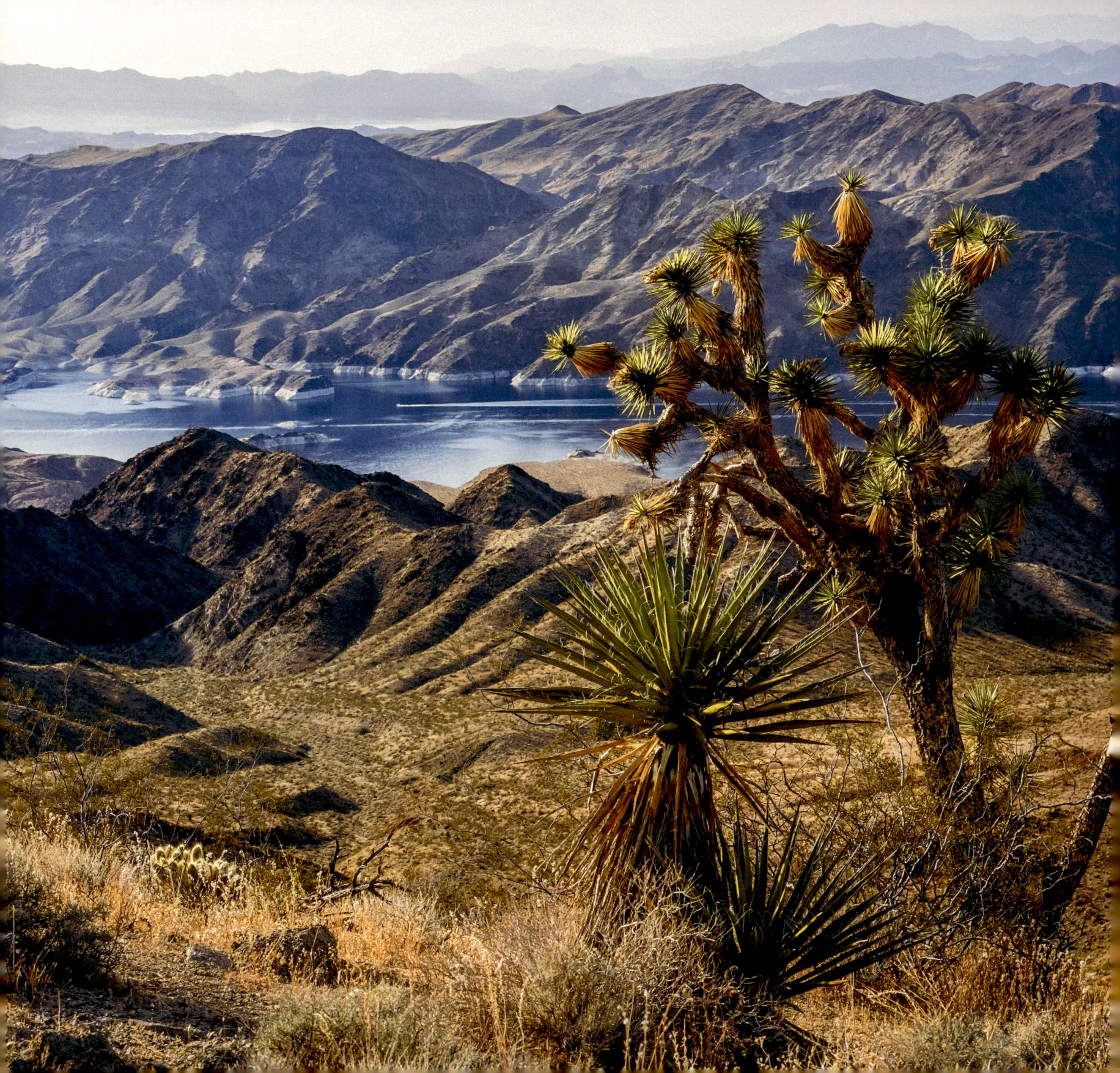

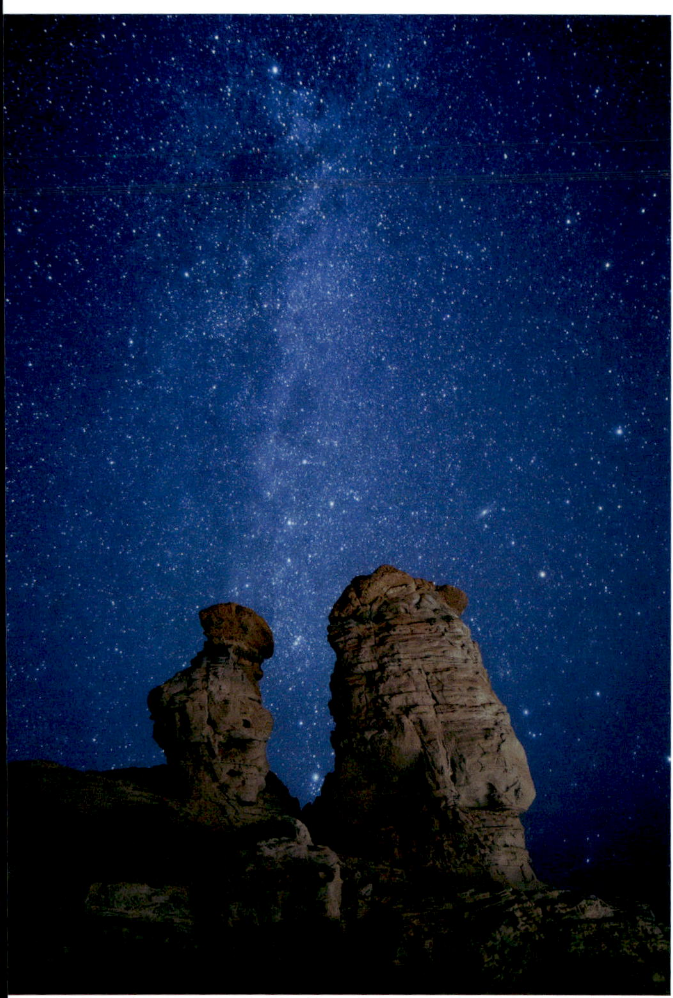

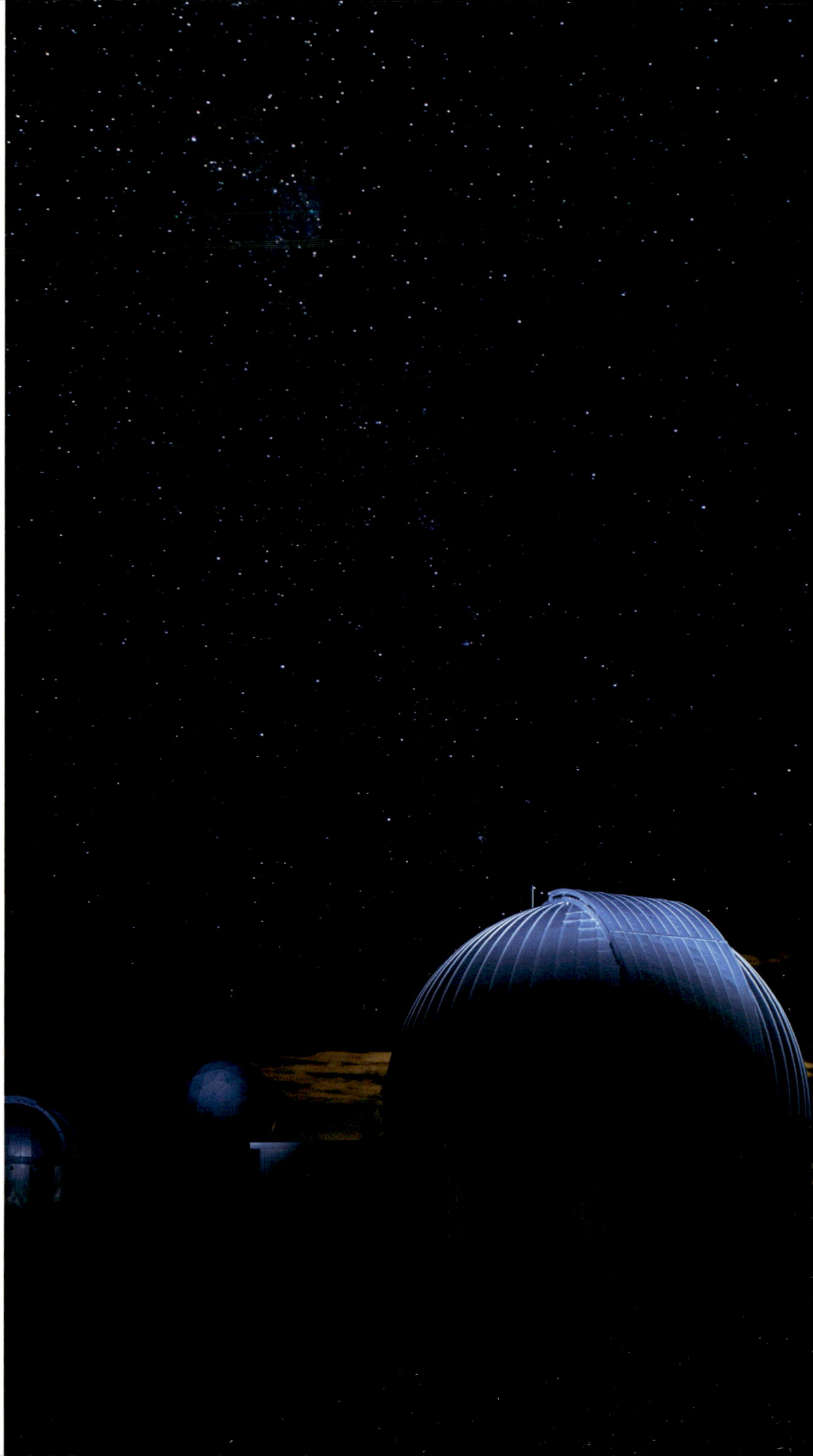

Above: The Milky Way Galaxy shines over a pair of sandstone hoodoos in Glen Canyon National Recreation Area. JAKE CASE

Right: Mount Lemmon Skycenter and Observatory offers reservation-only tours and stargazing at 9,157 feet above sea level in the Santa Catalina Mountains near Tucson. LARRY LINDAHL

Facing page: The deep night sky showcases the Milky Way behind ancient Wukoki Pueblo at Wupatki National Monument. The Sinagua culture structures sit near present-day Flagstaff which restricts light pollution and was honored as the first International Dark Sky City in 2001. LARRY LINDAHL

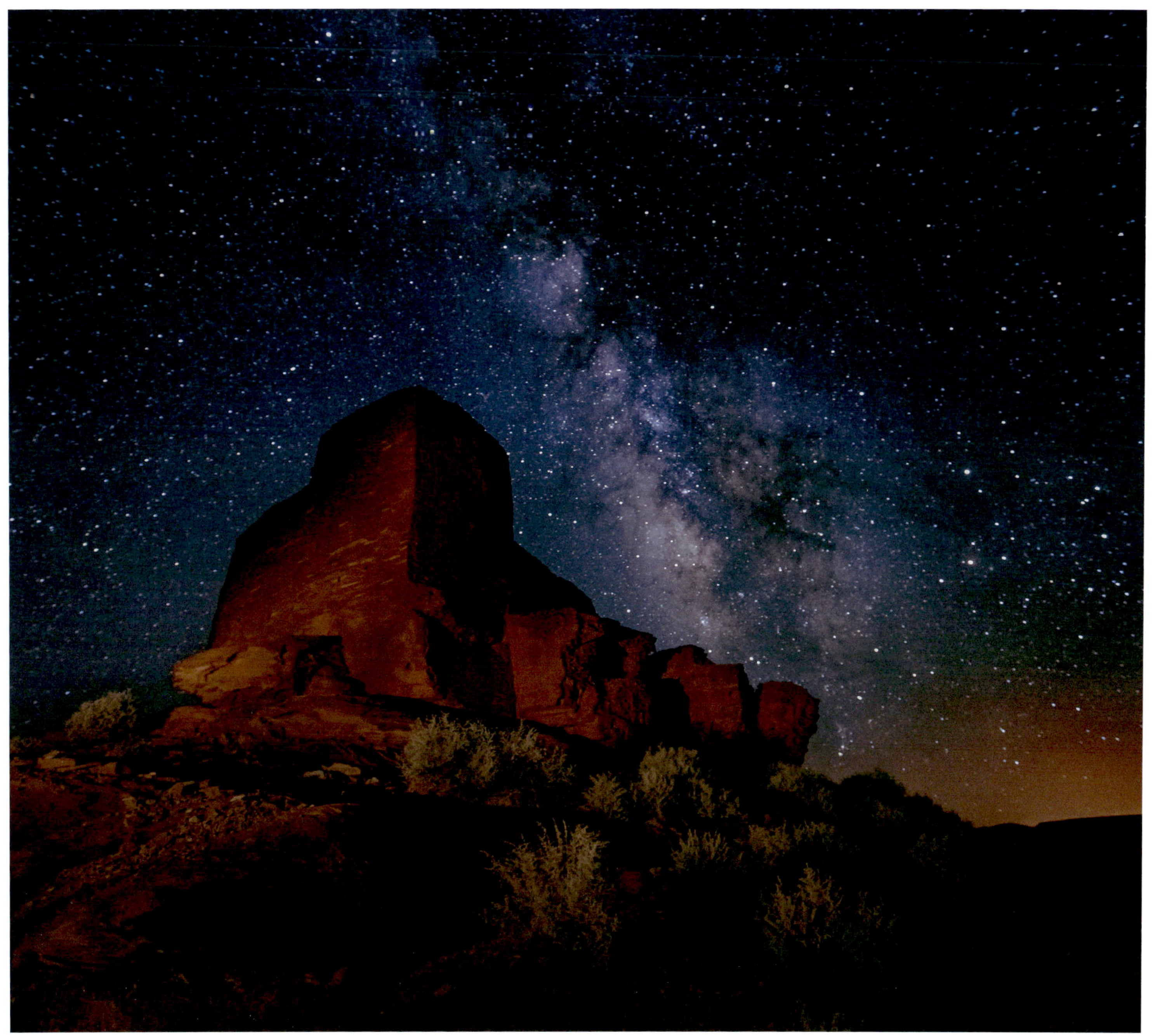

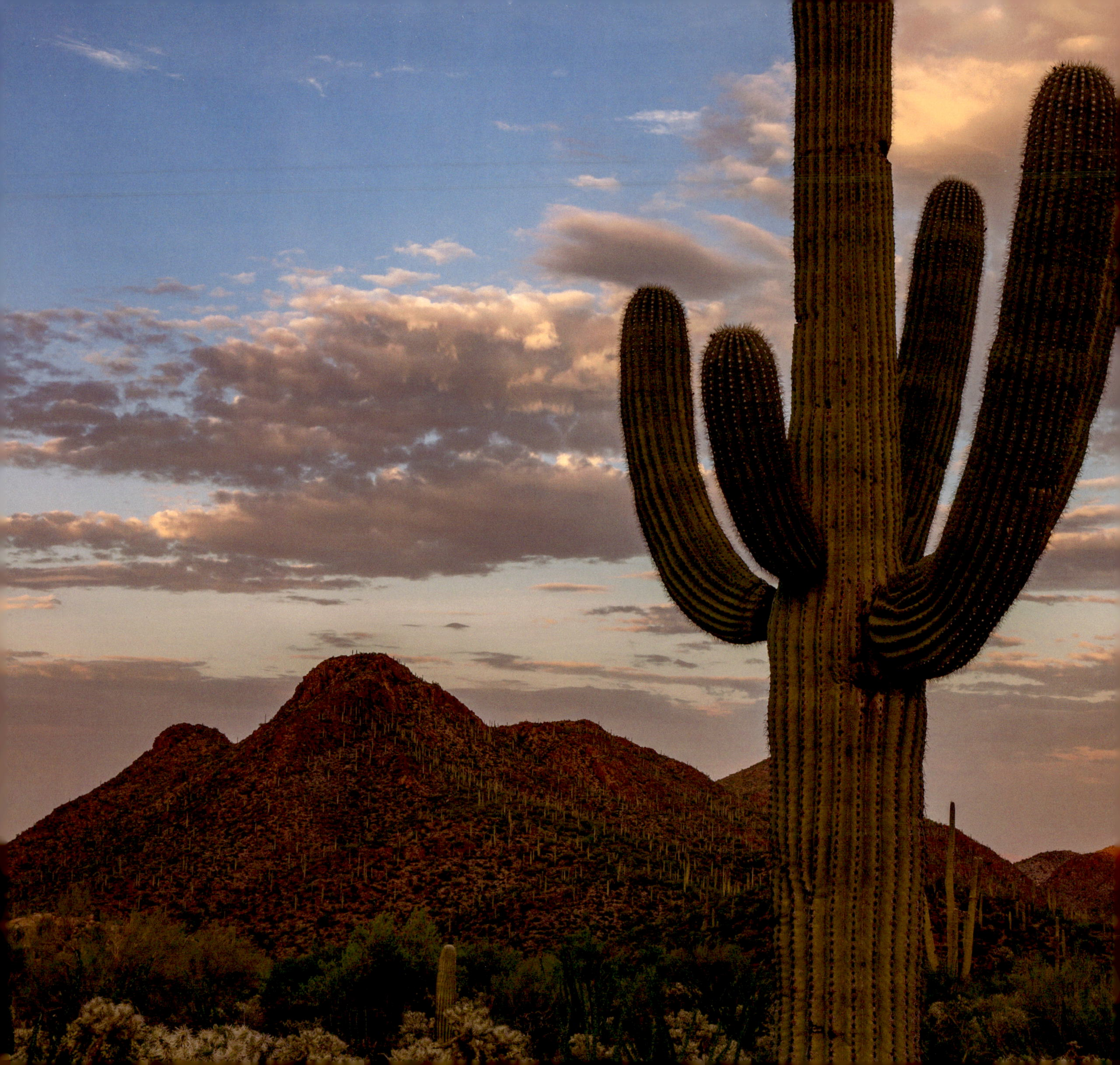

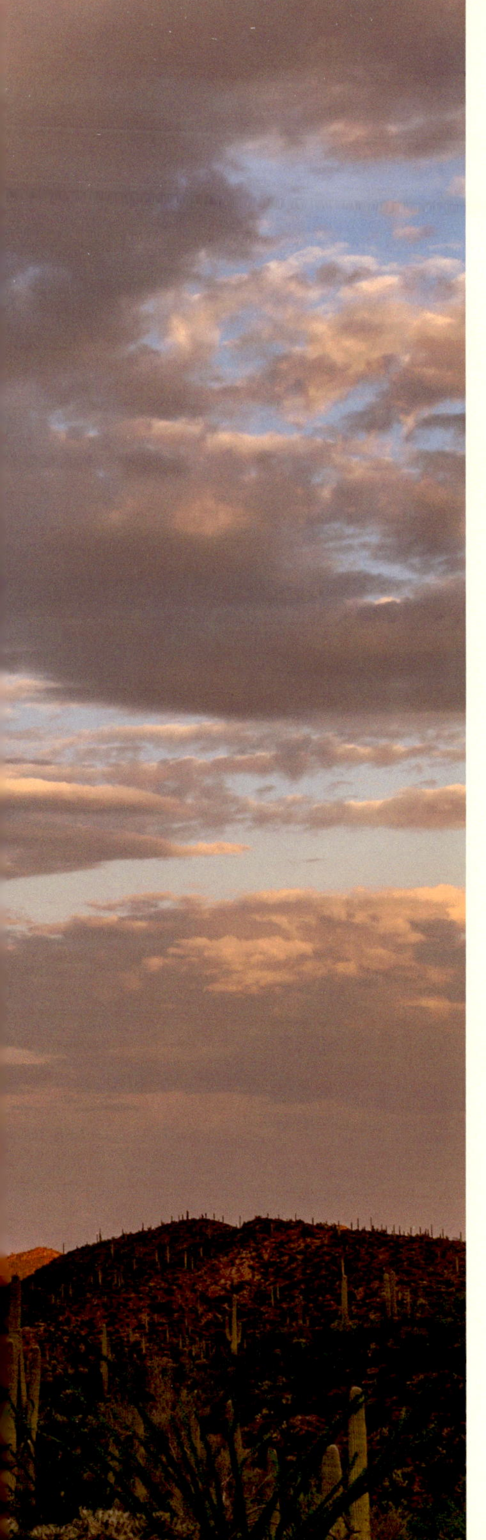

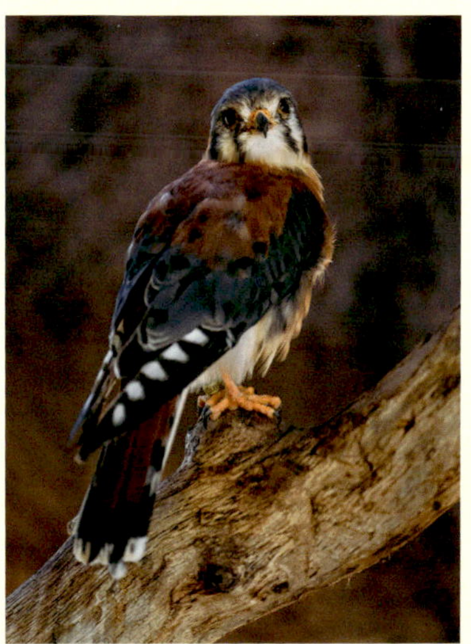

Left and below: Near Tucson, the Arizona-Sonora Desert Museum and Zoo is home to a wide variety of animals, such as this American kestrel and mountain lion. LARRY LINDAHL

Far left: The largest cactus of the United States, saguaros are slow growing. A decade-old saguaro may be less than 2 inches tall. LARRY LINDAHL

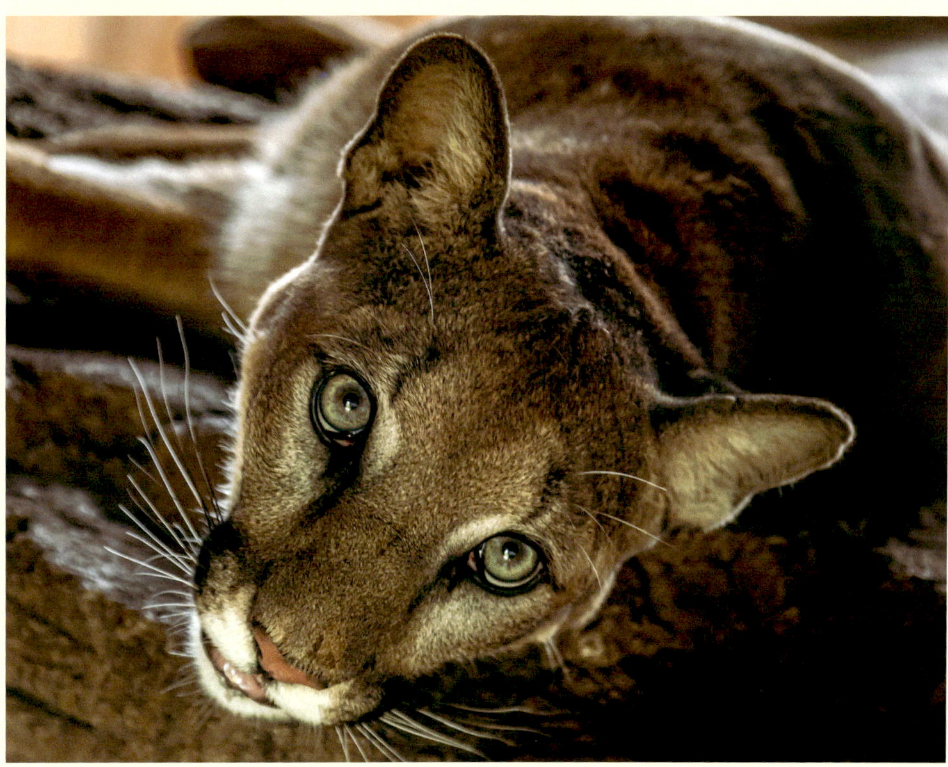

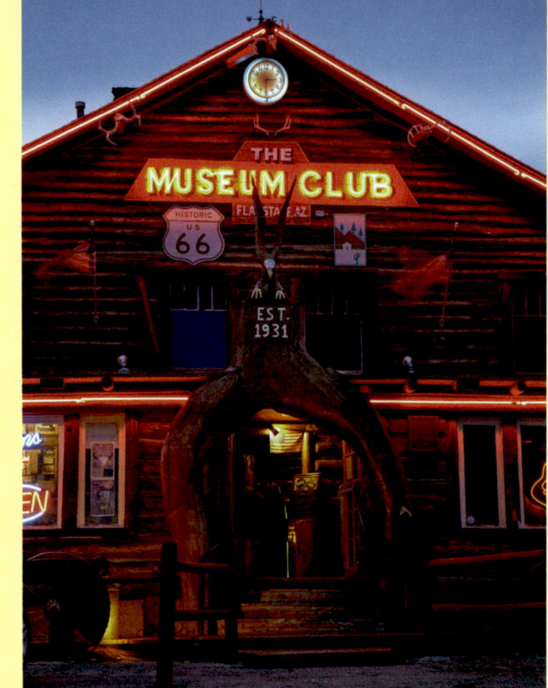

Right: On the east end of Flagstaff, The Museum Club, built in 1931, is a popular country-western roadhouse and dance hall on Historic Route 66. LARRY LINDAHL

Far right: Motorcycle riders lean into the curves while descending Gold Hill on Historic Route 66 (Oatman Highway) between Oatman and the California border. LARRY LINDAHL

Below: Hackberry General Store, built in 1934, sits on a lonely stretch of Historic Route 66 east of Kingman. LARRY LINDAHL

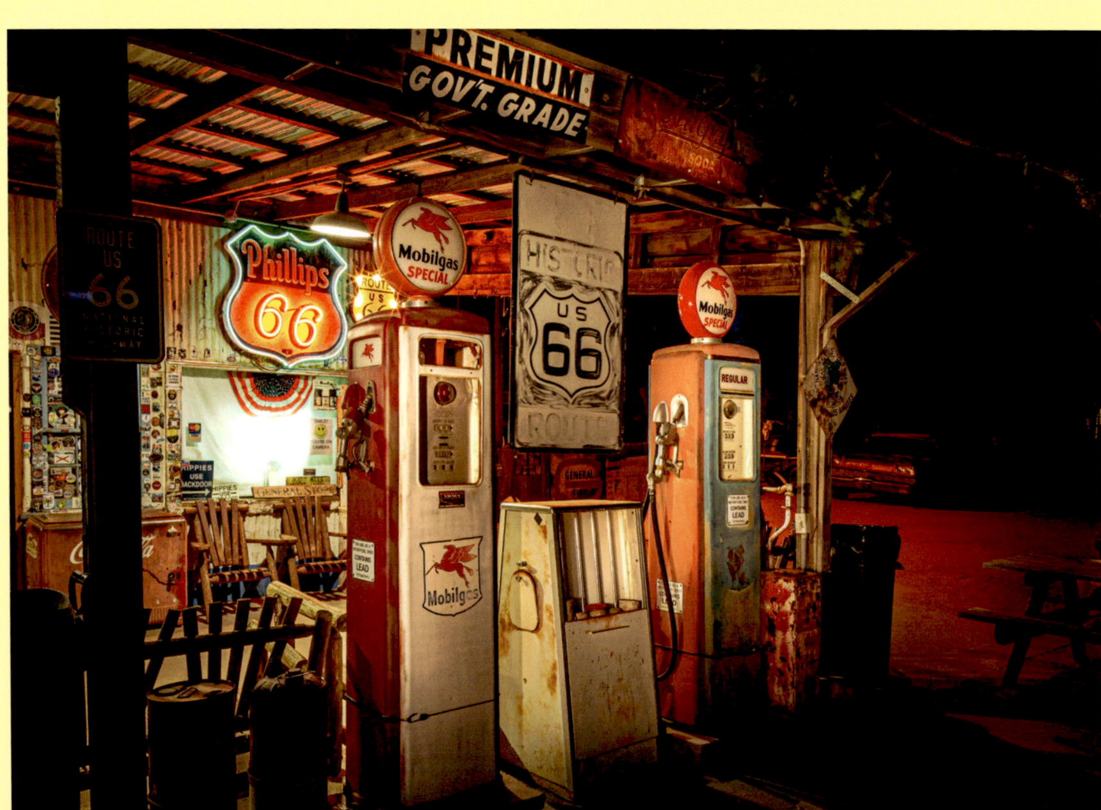

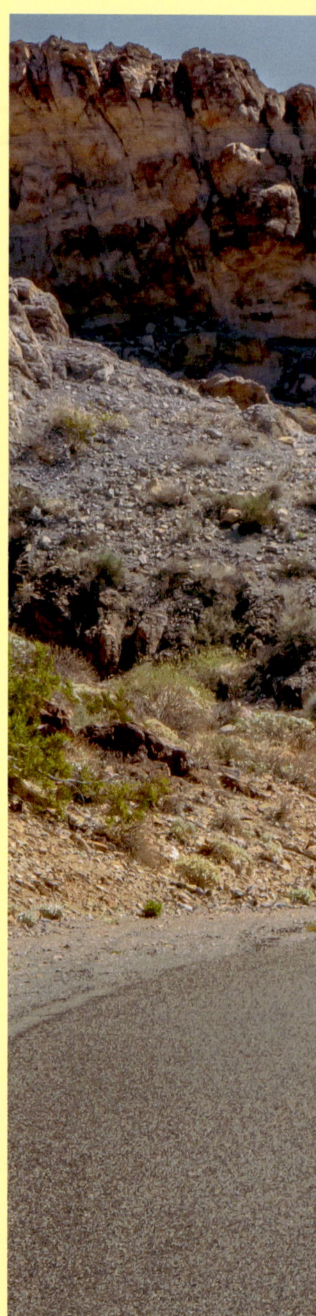

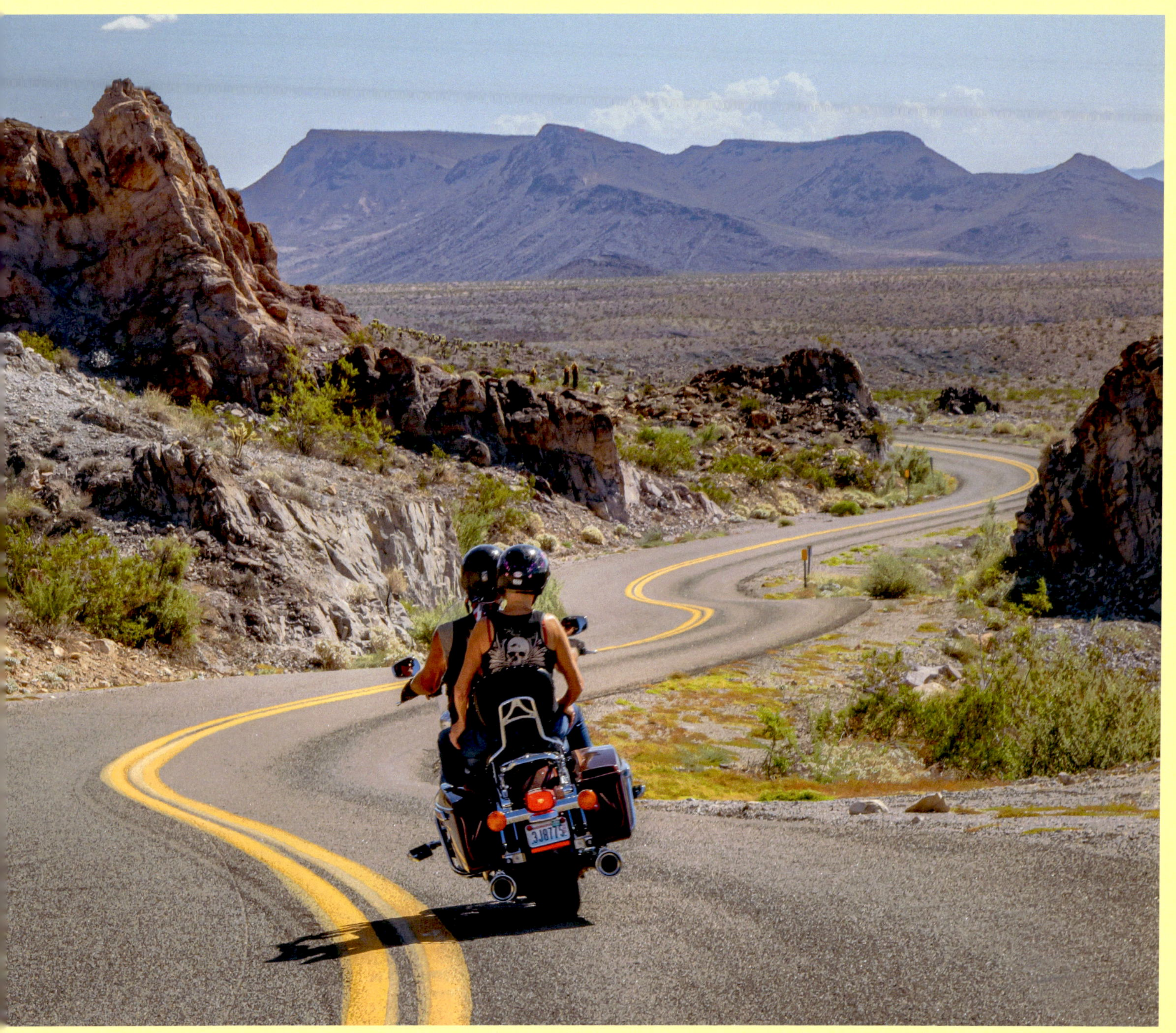
3J8775

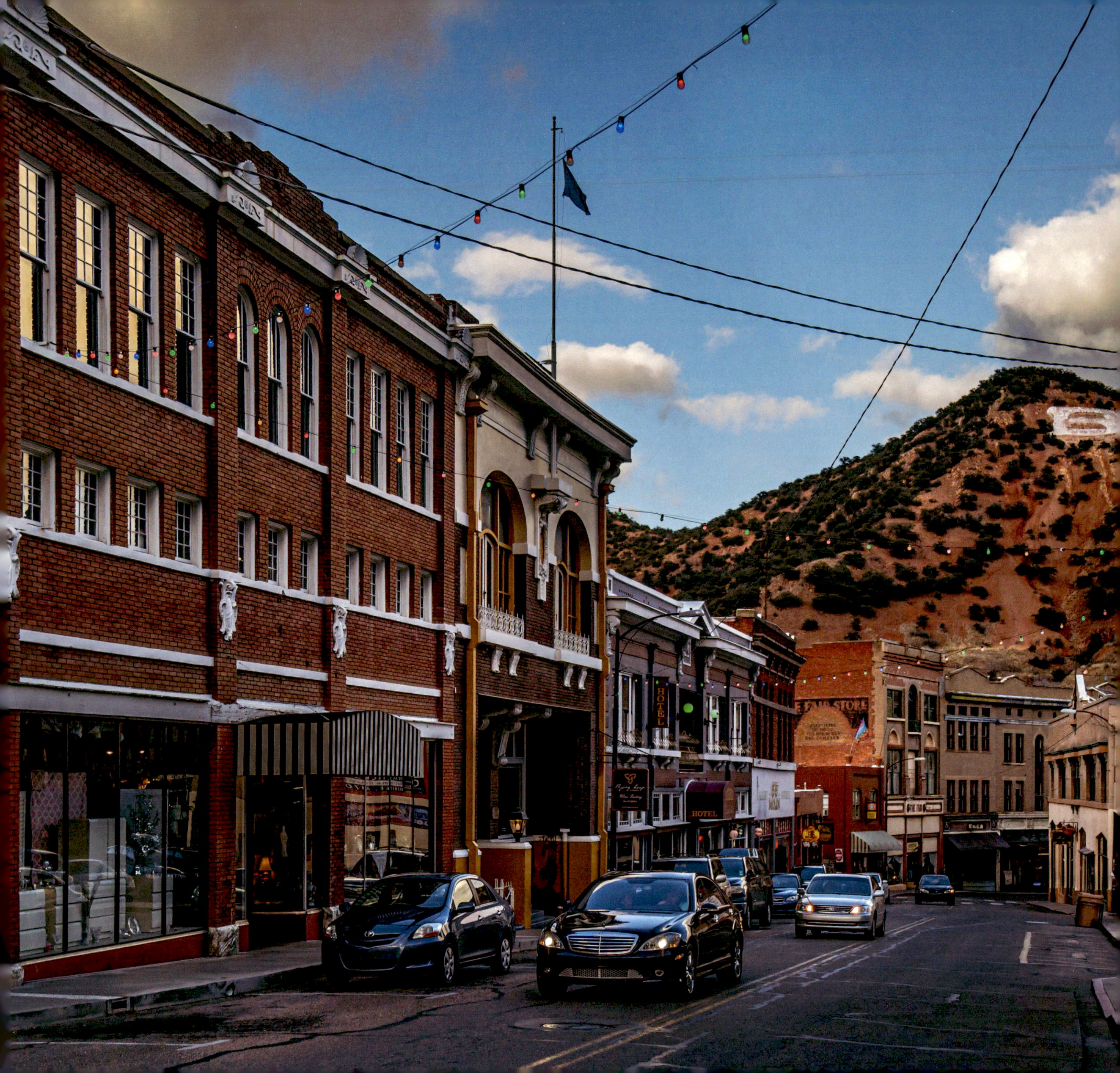
HOTEL
HOTEL

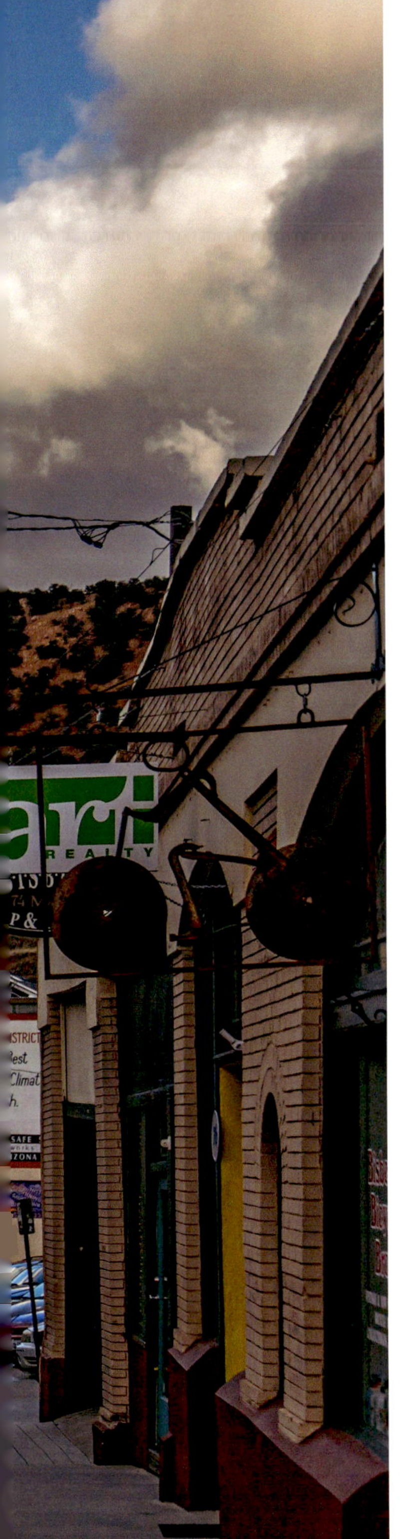

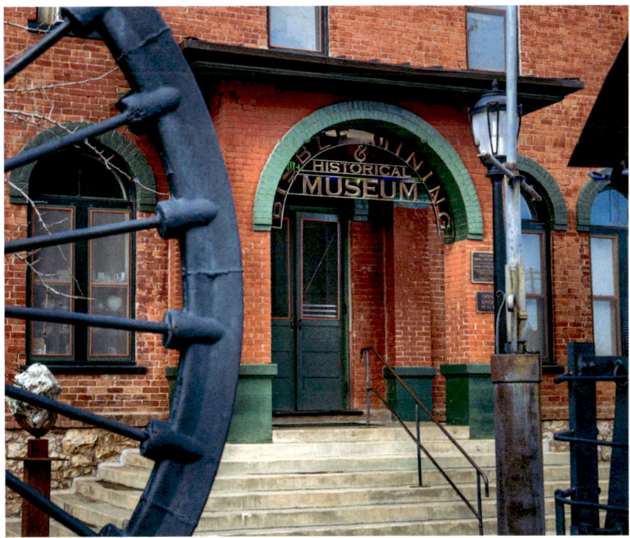

Left: A Smithsonian affiliate, the Bisbee Mining and Historical Museum offers award-winning interactive exhibits that explain copper mining and the American Industrial Revolution. LARRY LINDAHL

Far left: Art galleries, shops, and restaurants line the main street of Bisbee, a former copper mining town. LARRY LINDAHL

Below: Touring the Queen Mine in Bisbee, visitors wear miners' helmets and headlamps. LARRY LINDAHL

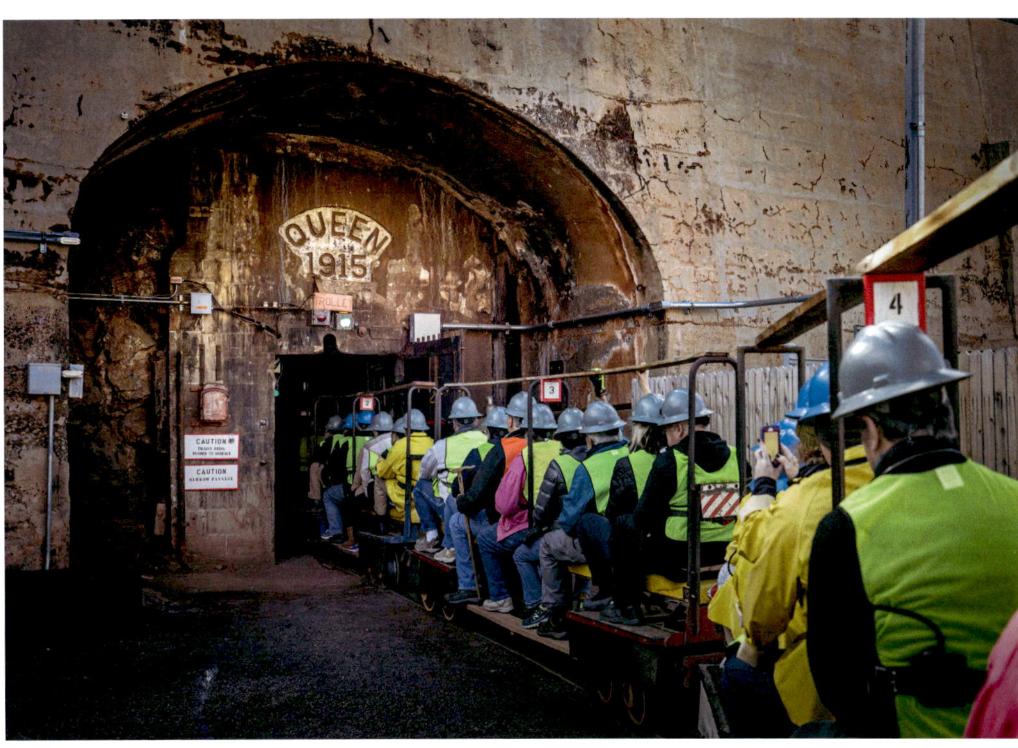

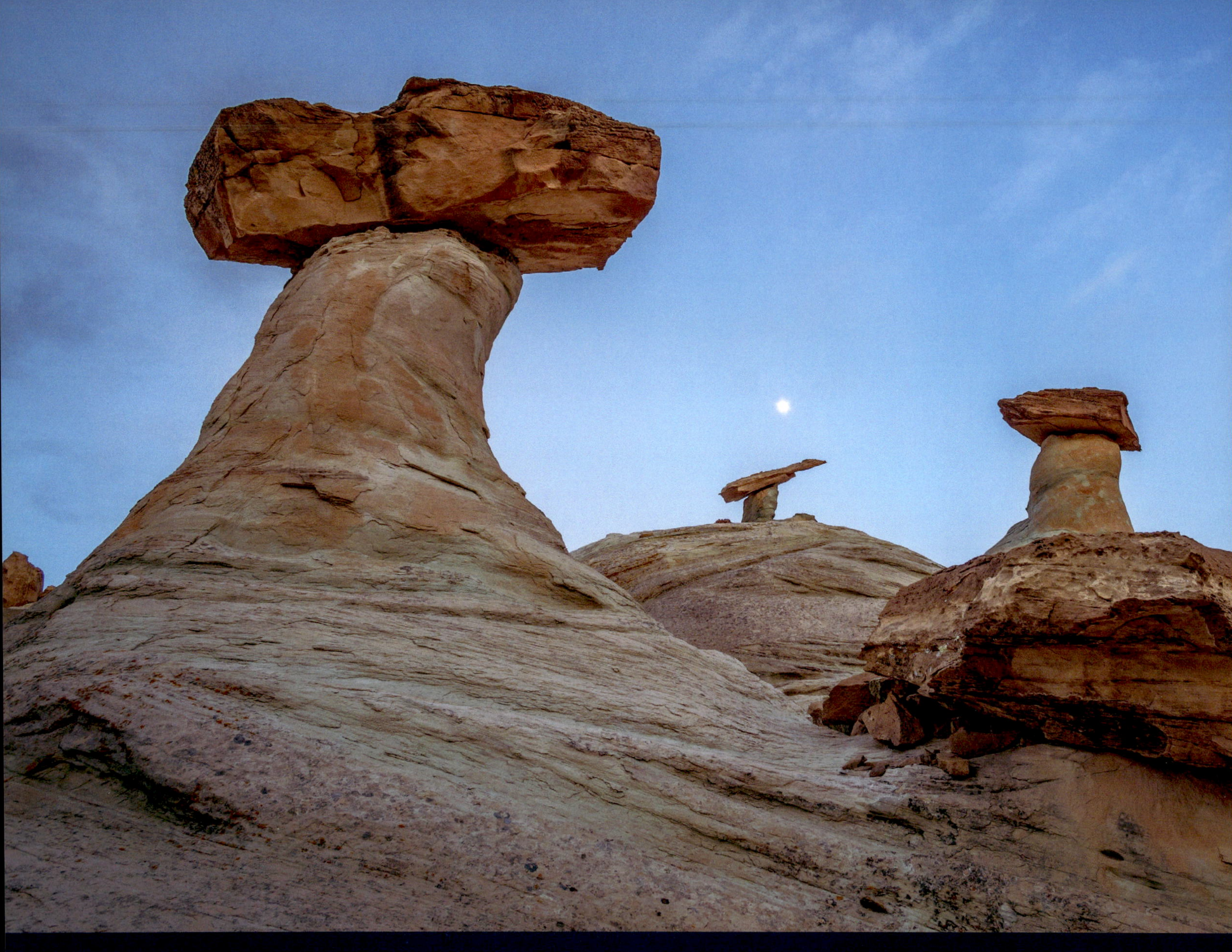

Above: A waxing gibbous moon rises over the balanced rocks at Stud Horse Point just south of the Arizona-Utah border. JAKE CASE

Facing page: Sitting atop the Mogollon Rim at 7,500 feet above sea level, Woods Canyon Lake reflects a brilliant summer sunrise. JAKE CASE

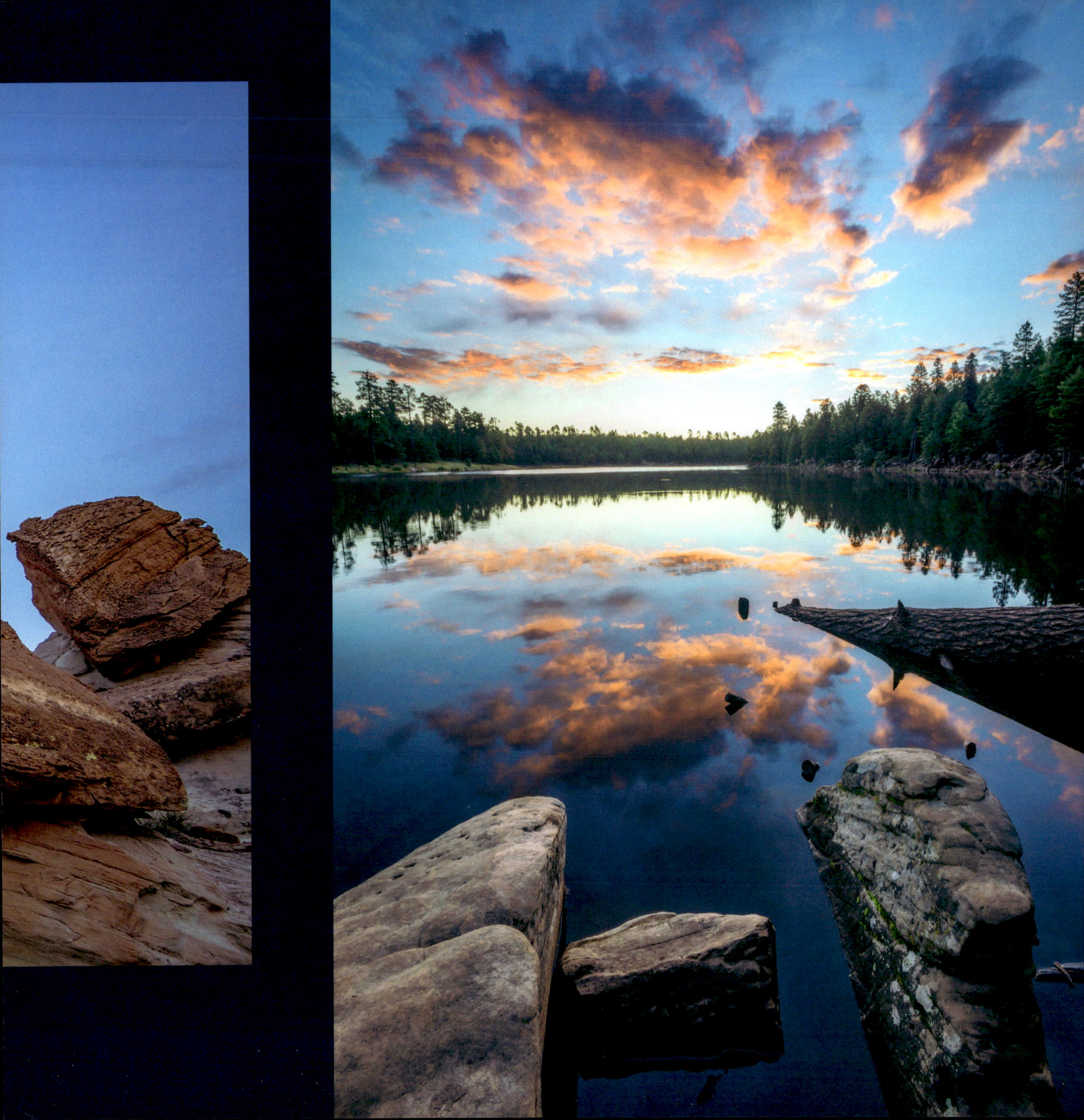

Right: Hopi katsina figures, like *Shalako Taka* carved by Edward Seechoma from Hotevilla, Third Mesa, are used to educate Hopi girls about spirit guides and the Hopi belief system. LARRY LINDAHL

Far right: Rooms glow with sunrise at the Upper Cliff Dwelling of the ancient Salado culture at Tonto National Monument. LARRY LINDAHL

Below: Sagebrush dots the high desert plain surrounding Wukoki Pueblo, a 900-year-old ruin in Wupatki National Monument. The Hopi people believe the building's former occupants remain here as spiritual guardians. JAKE CASE

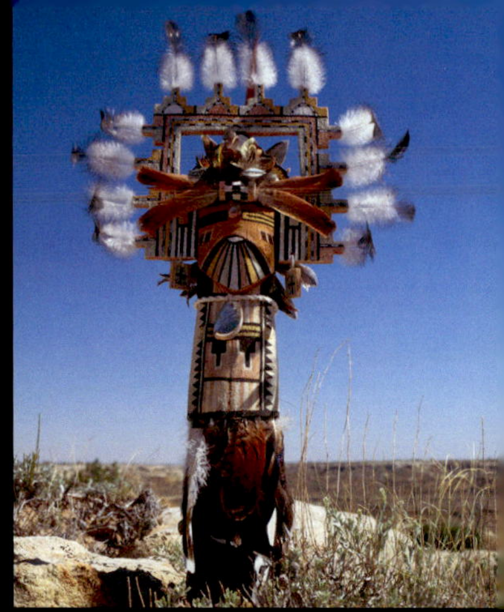

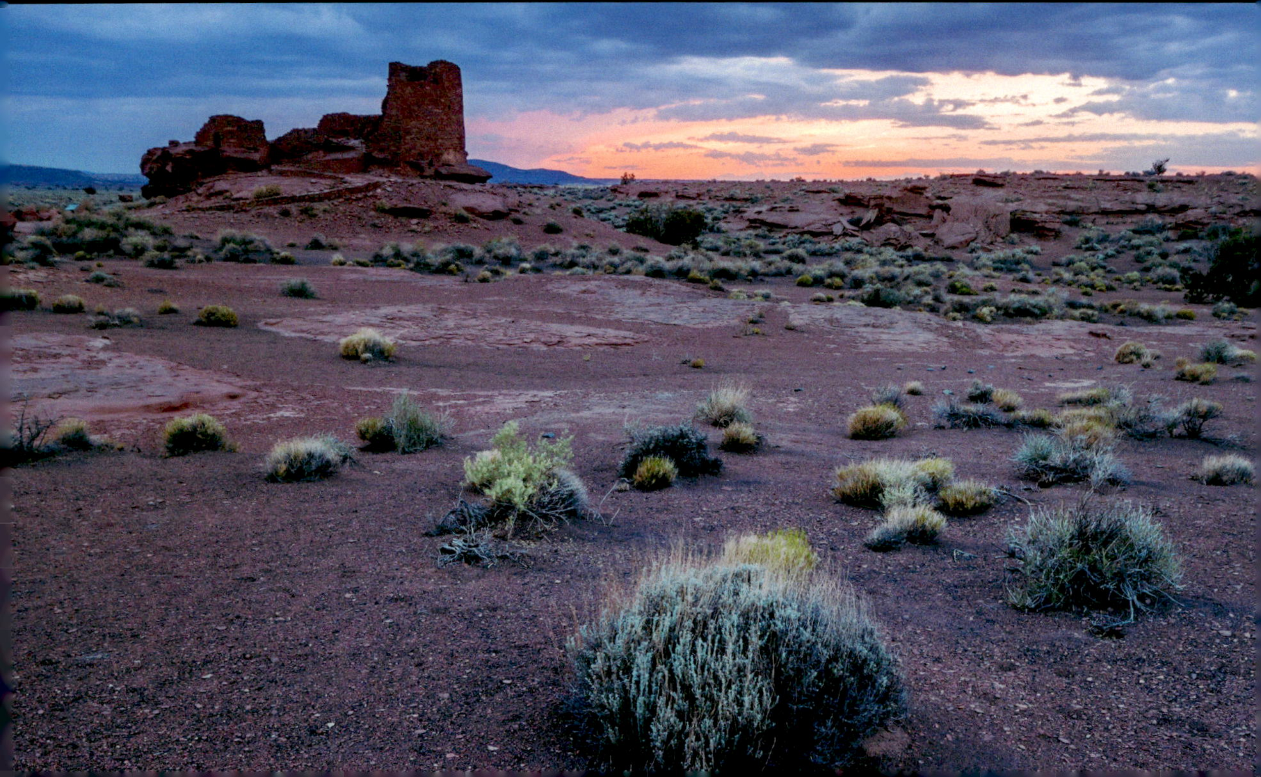

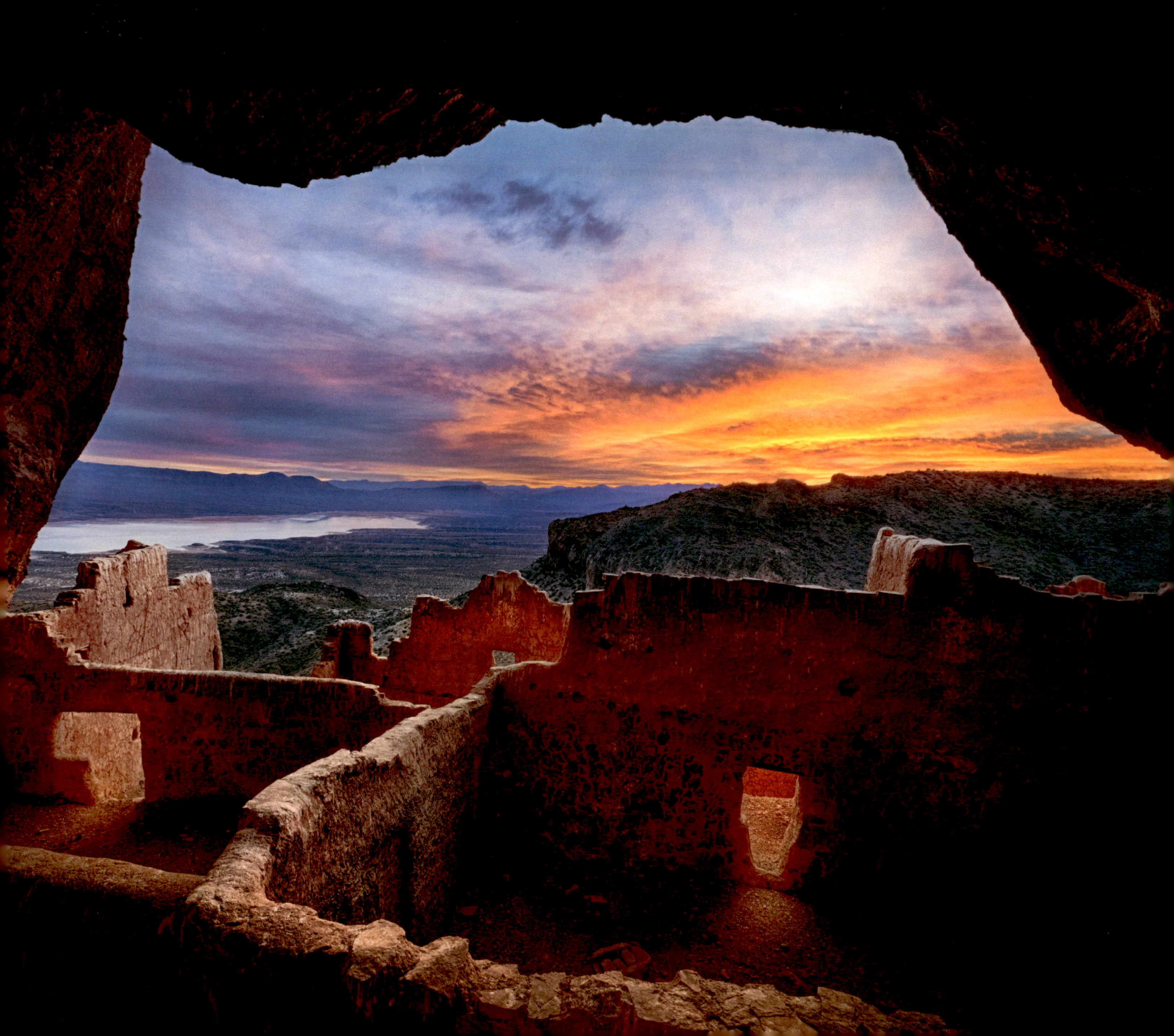

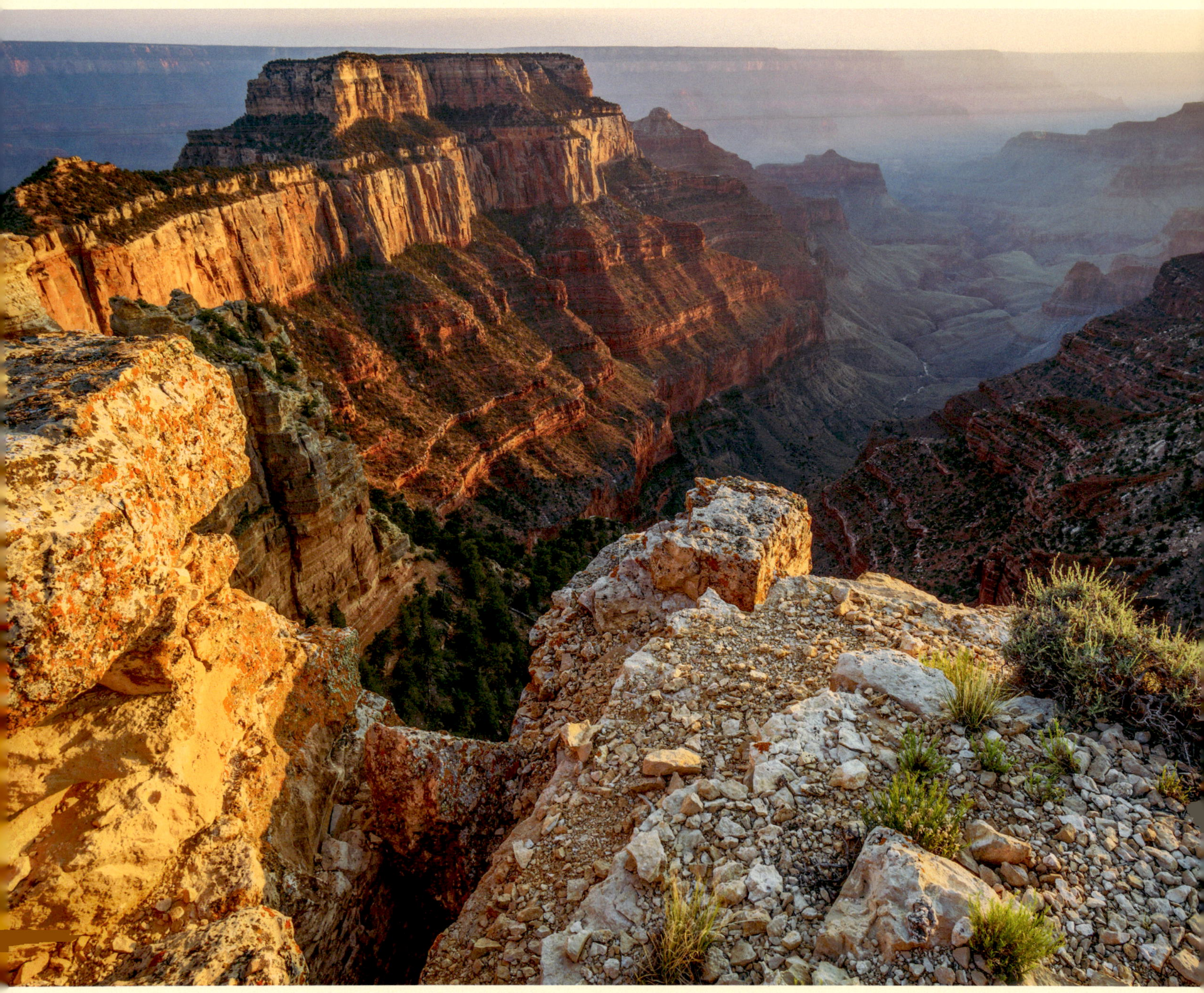

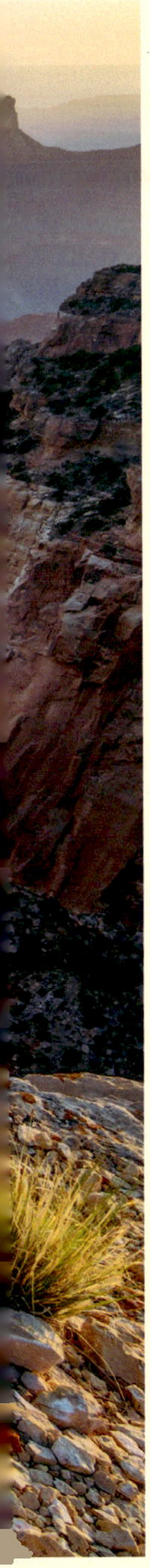

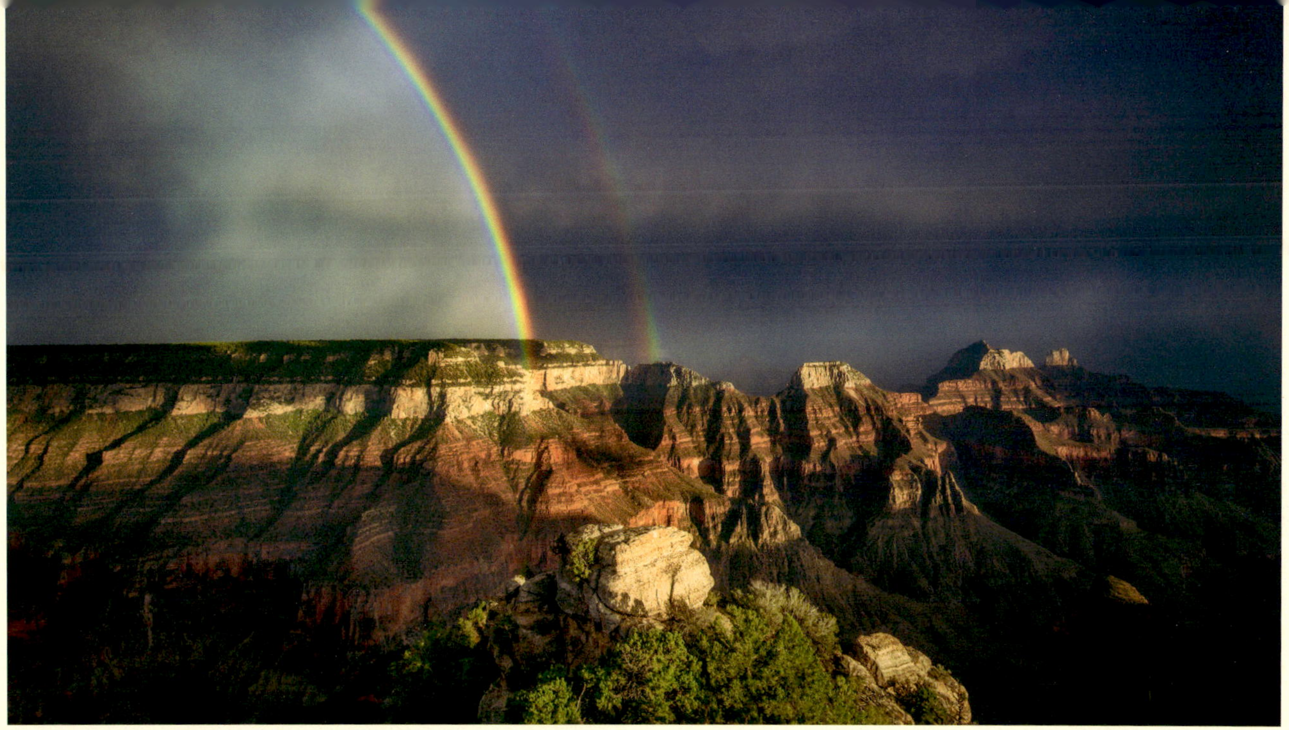

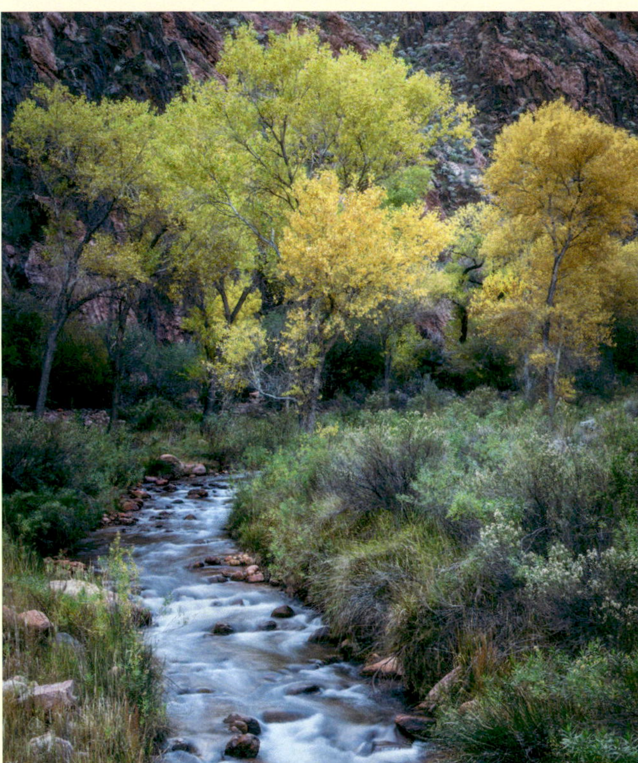

Above: A double-rainbow shimmers during a break in a summer monsoon at the Grand Canyon North Rim's Bright Angel Point. JAKE CASE

Left: December brings fall colors to the Fremont cottonwoods growing along Bright Angel Creek in the depths of Grand Canyon National Park. JAKE CASE

Far left: The June sun pierces through hazy skies to illuminate Wotan's Throne as viewed from Cape Royal on the Grand Canyon North Rim. JAKE CASE

Right and below: Christmas decorations enliven the Tlaquepaque Arts and Crafts Village in Sedona. LARRY LINDAHL

Far right: Cathedral Rock basks in the setting sun, as seen from the picnic site at Crescent Moon Ranch near Sedona. LARRY LINDAHL

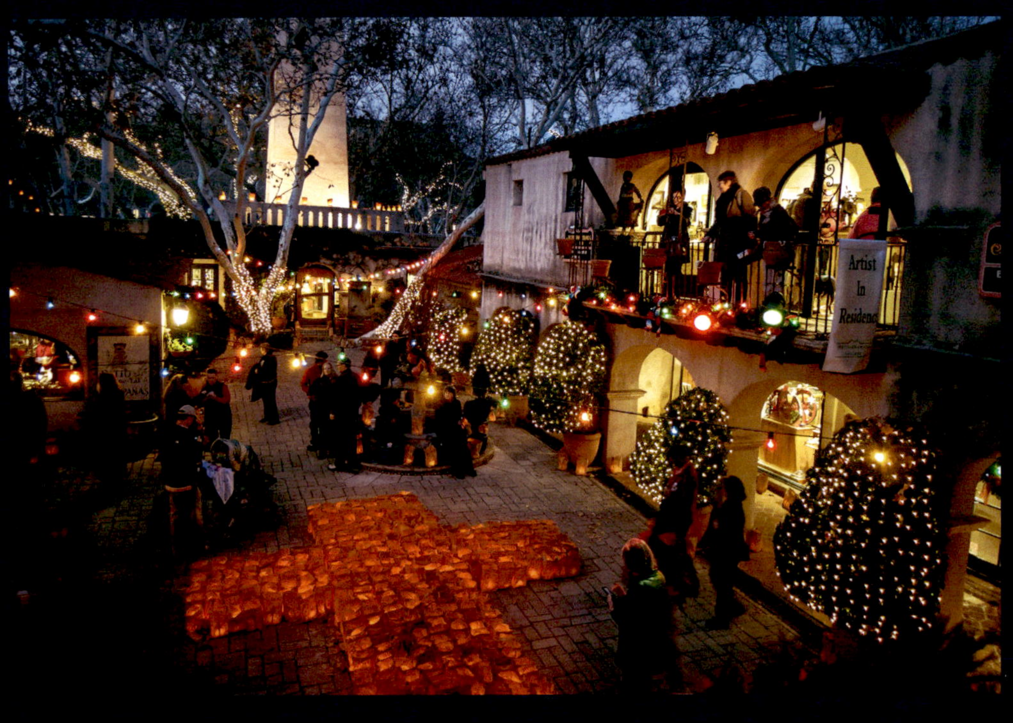

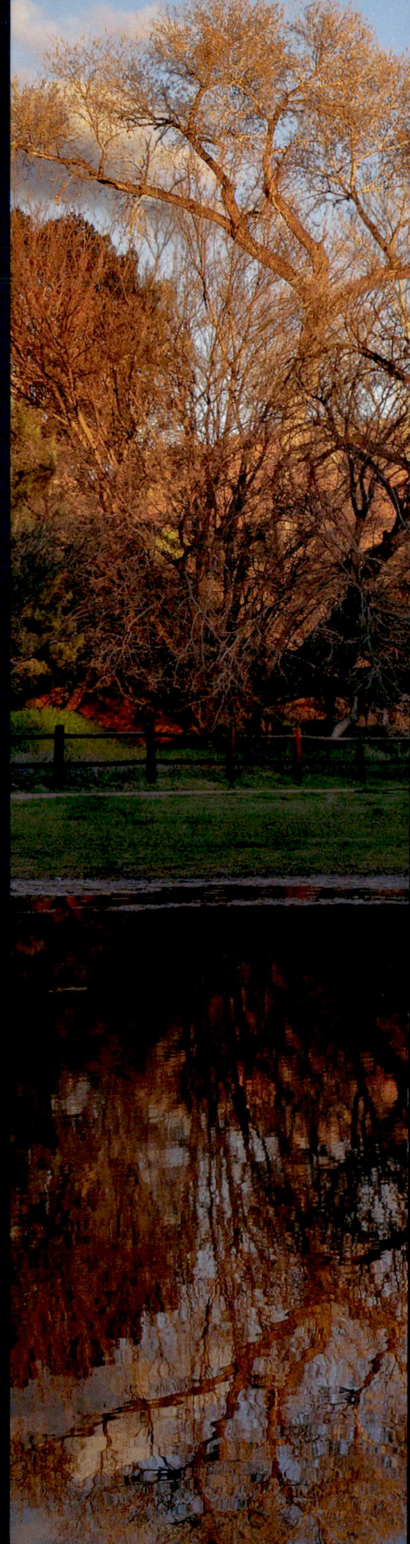

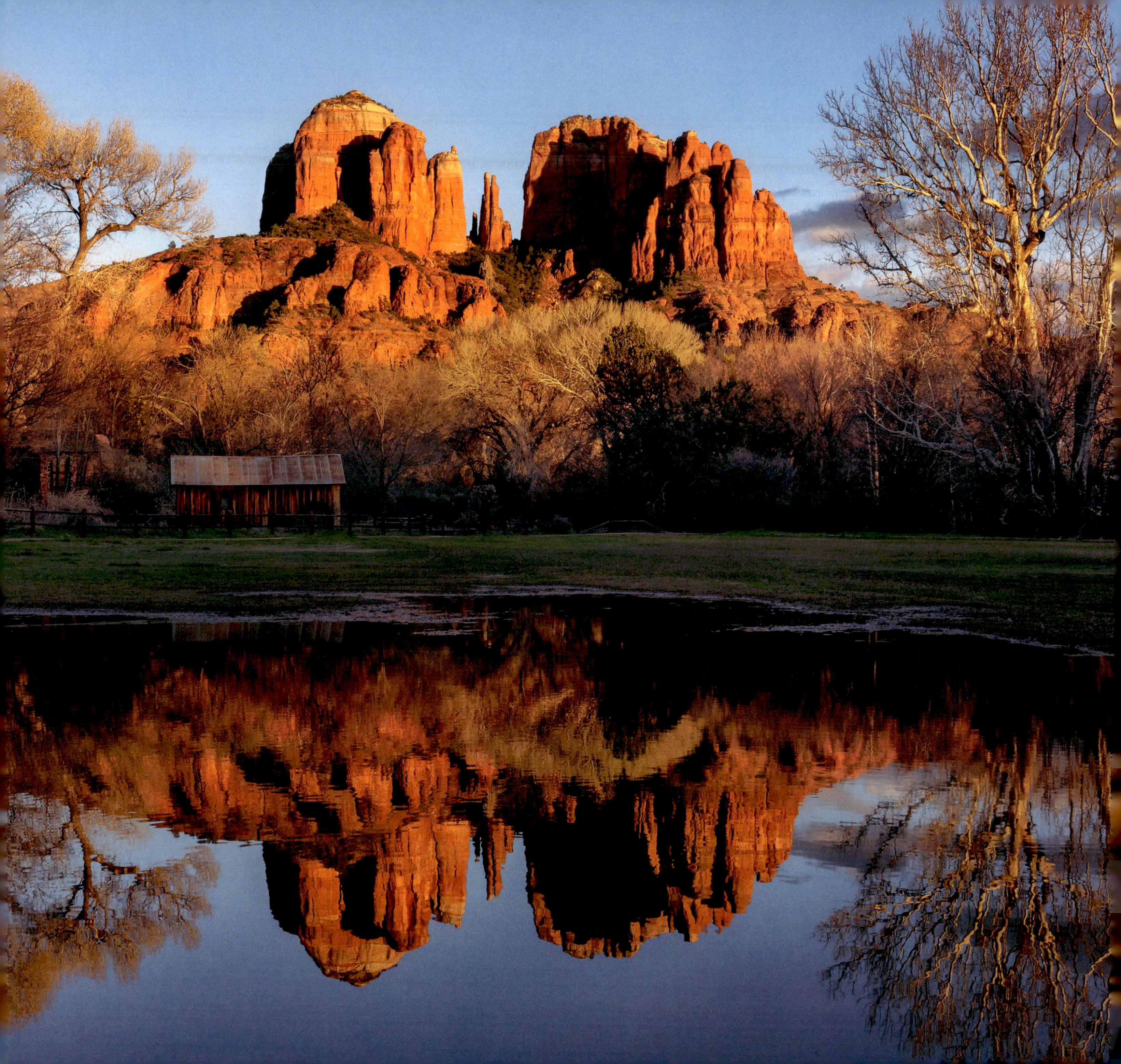

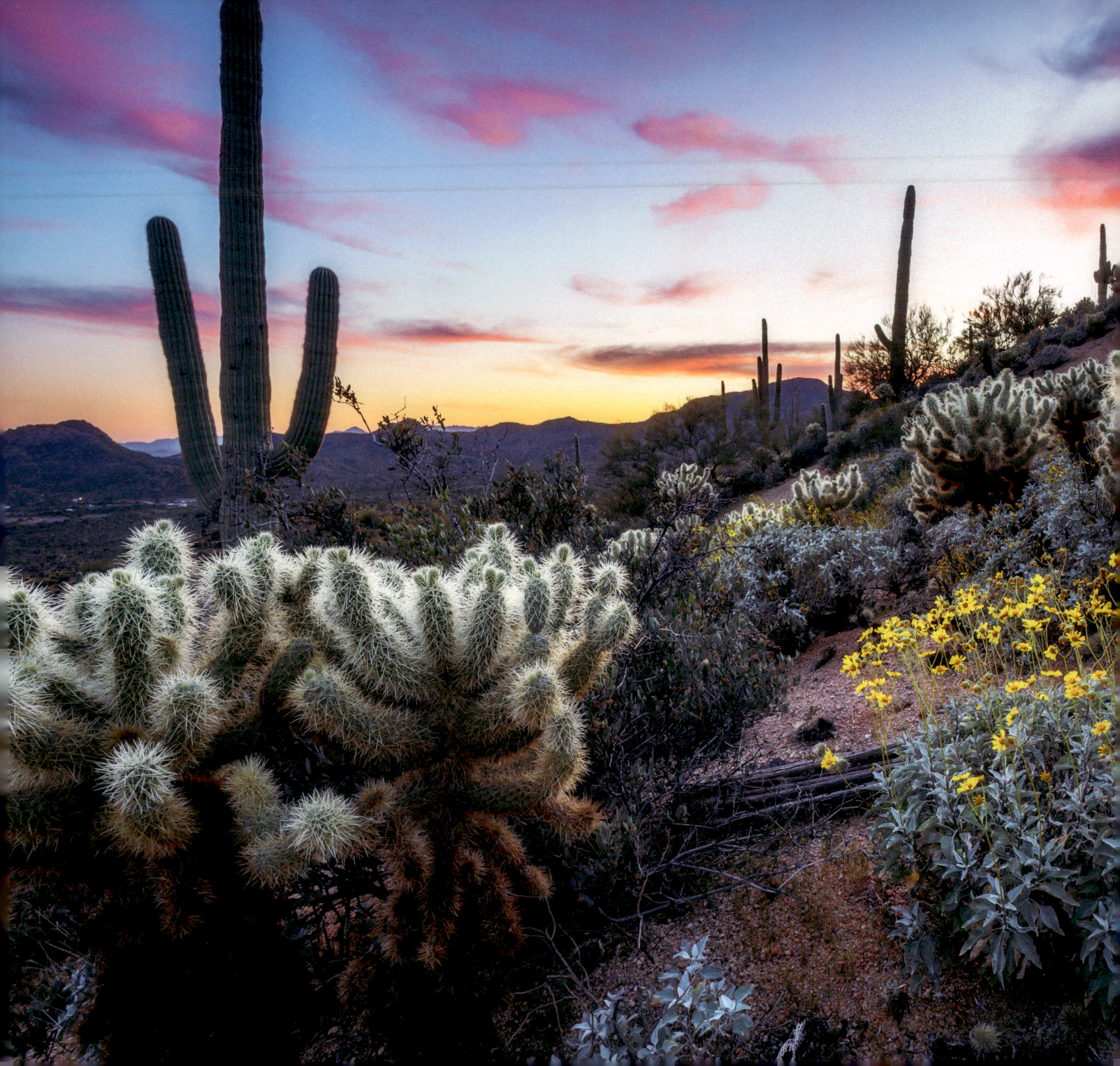

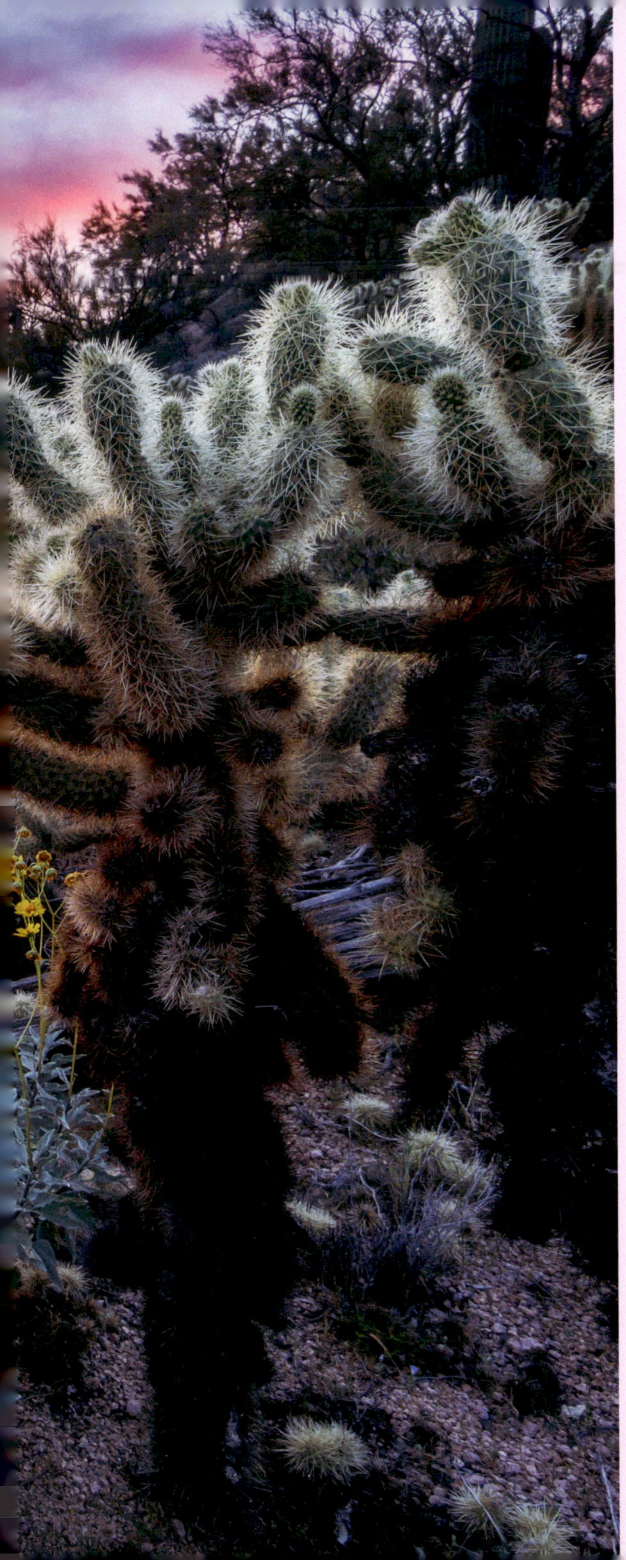

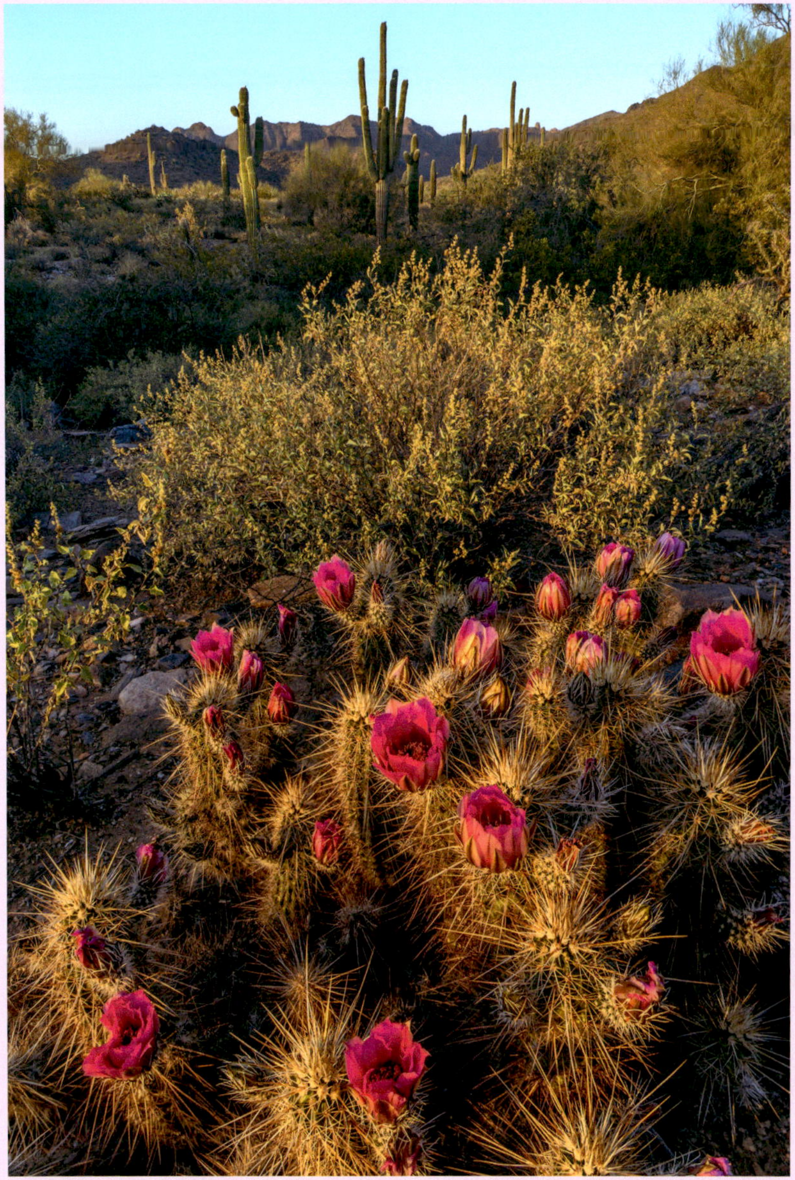

Above: Flowering Nichol's hedgehog cacti add a splash of vibrant color to Scottsdale's McDowell Mountains. JAKE CASE

Left: An April sunset paints the sky over saguaros, teddy bear cholla, and blooming brittlebush near Bartlett Lake. JAKE CASE

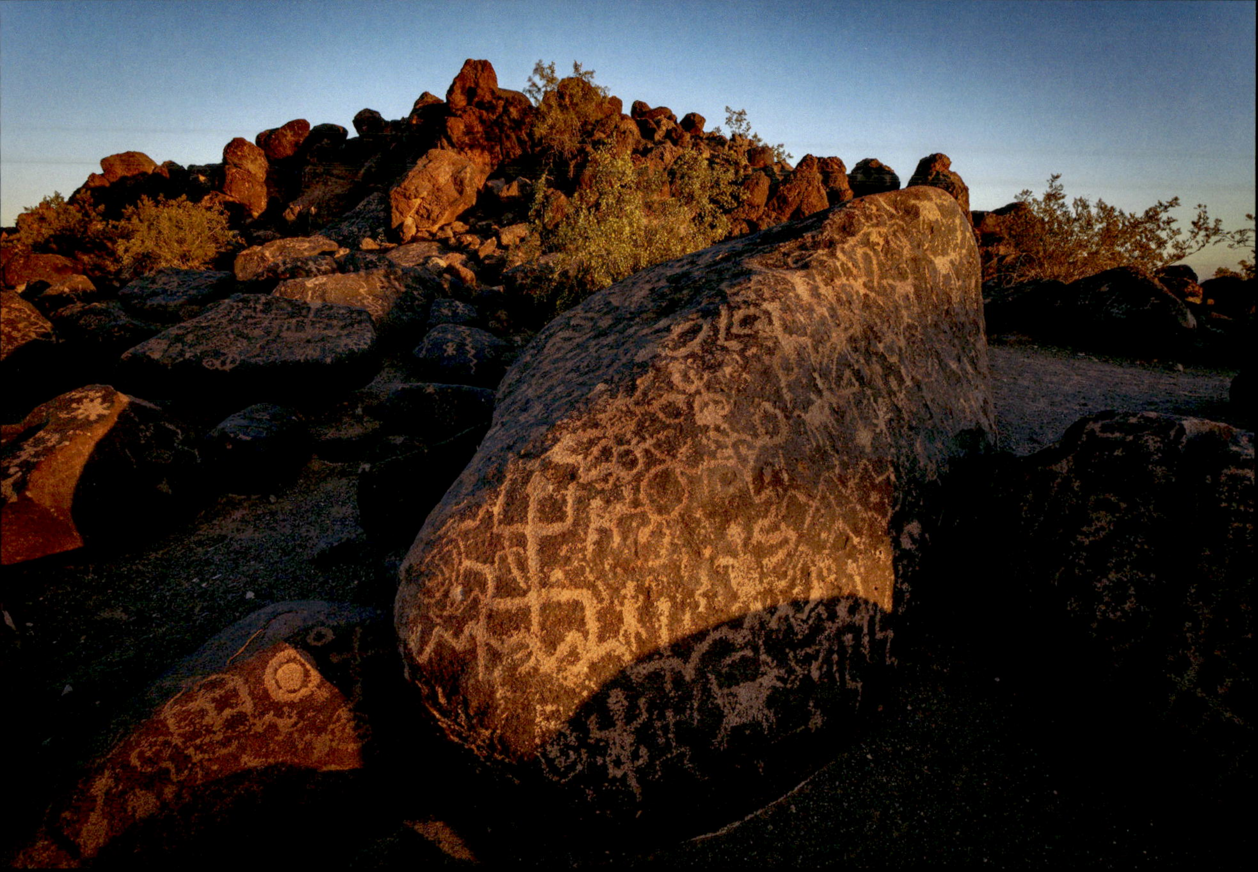

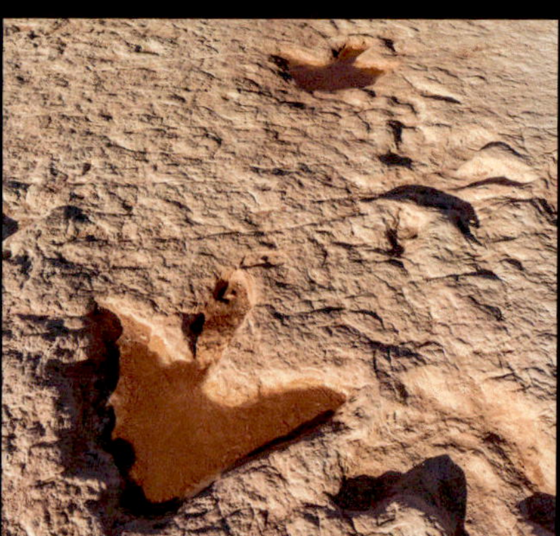

Above: Basalt boulders in the Gila River Valley showcase Hohokam culture rock art at Painted Rock Petroglyph Site northwest of Gila Bend. LARRY LINDAHL

Right: Dinosaur tracks from over 200 million years ago, near Tuba City. LARRY LINDAHL

Far right: An abandoned 1941 Plymouth coupe slowly rusts away in the Kofa Mountains between Quartzsite and Yuma. LARRY LINDAHL

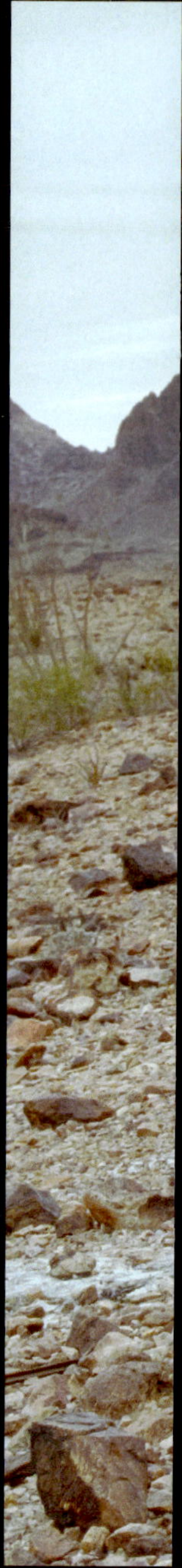

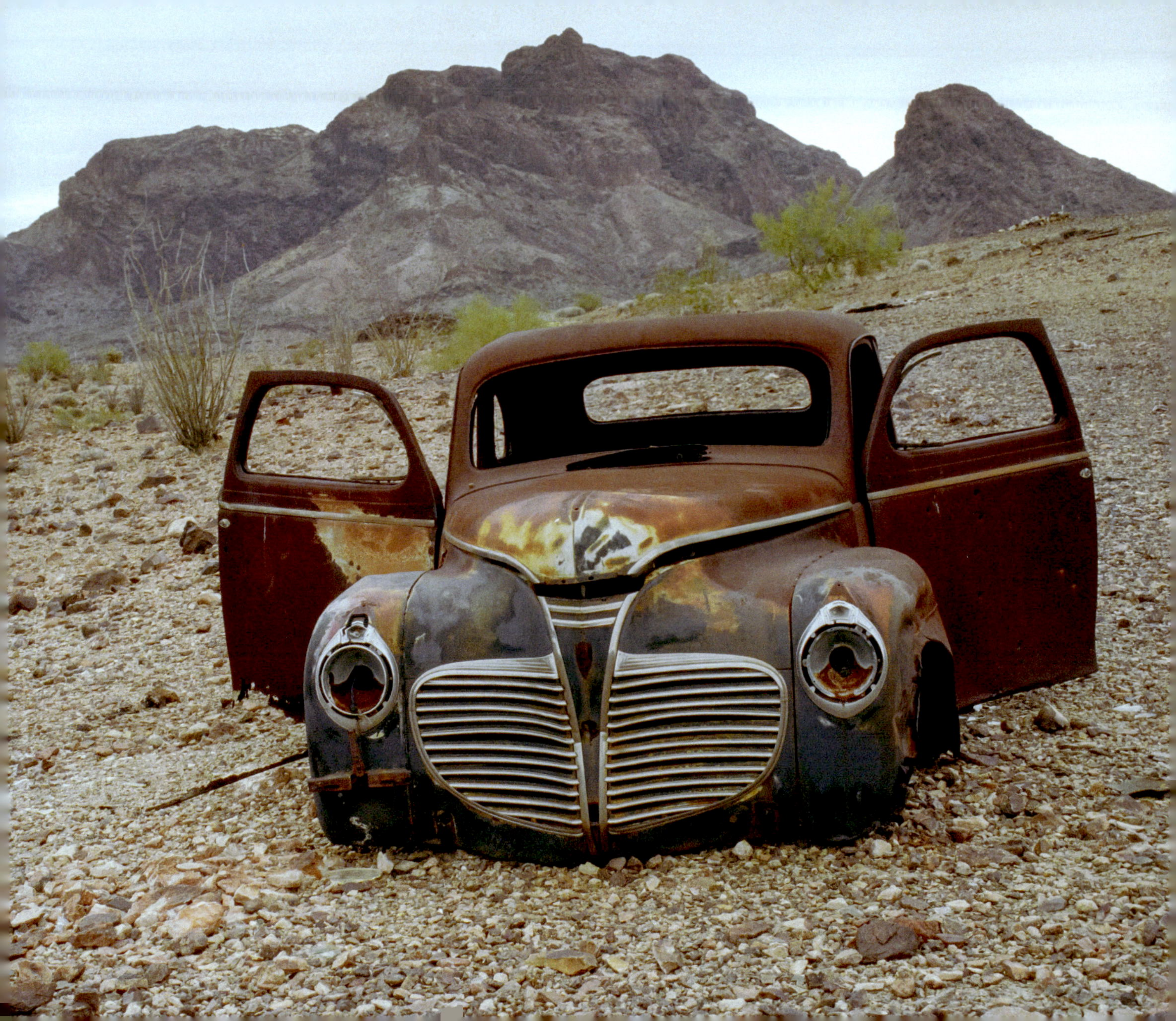

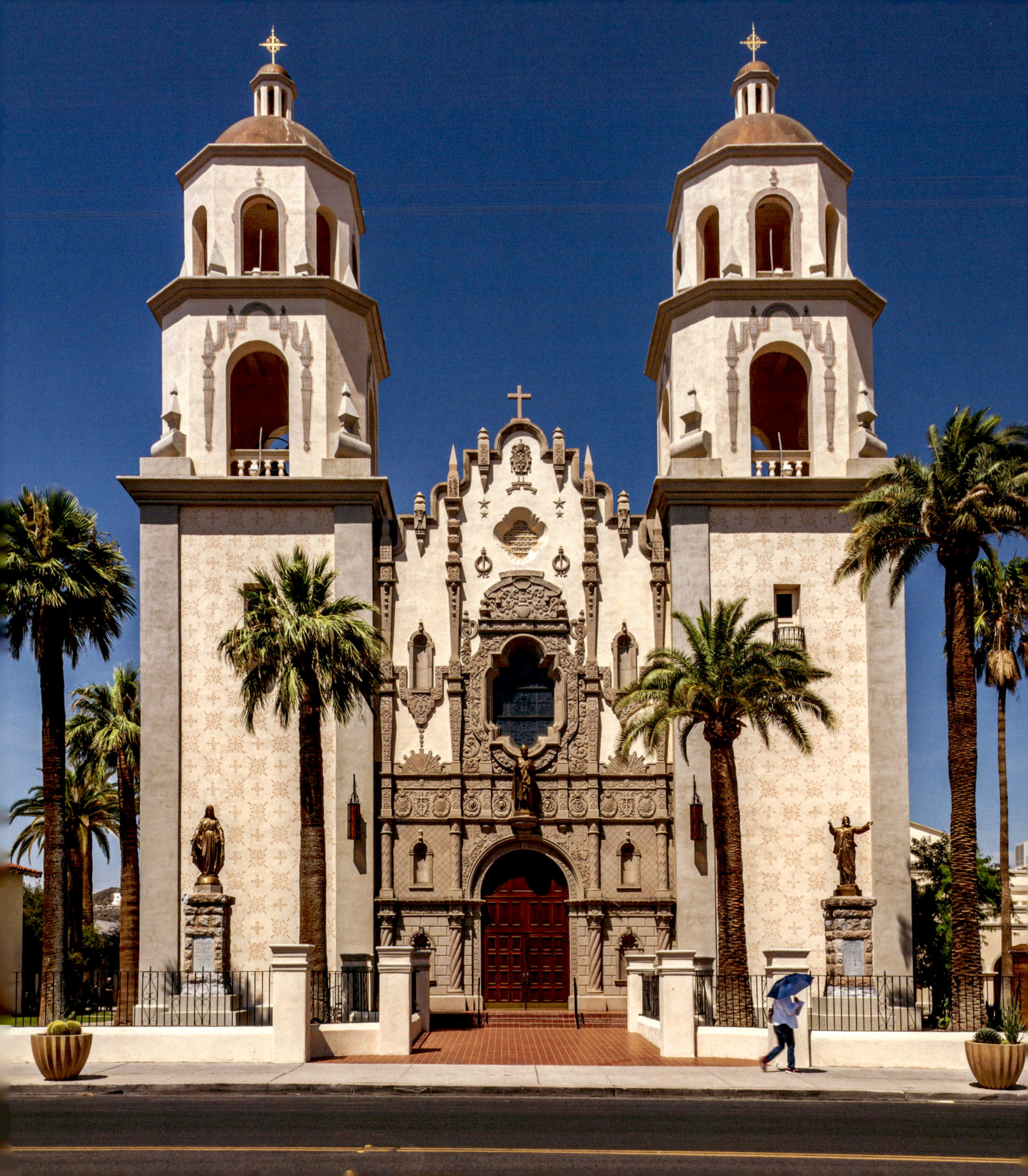

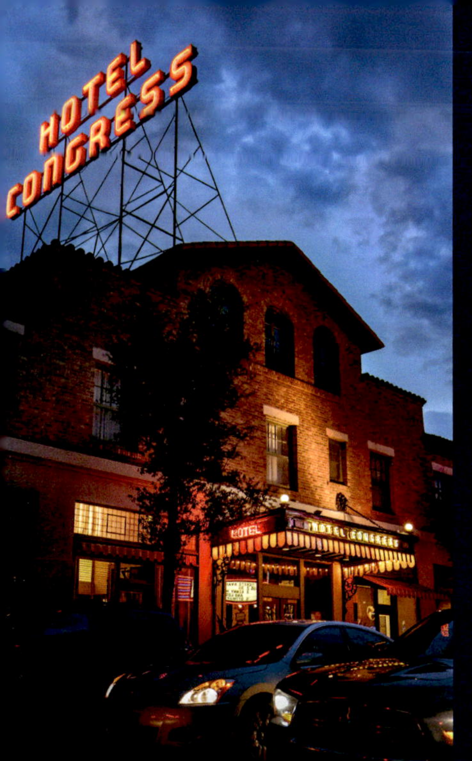

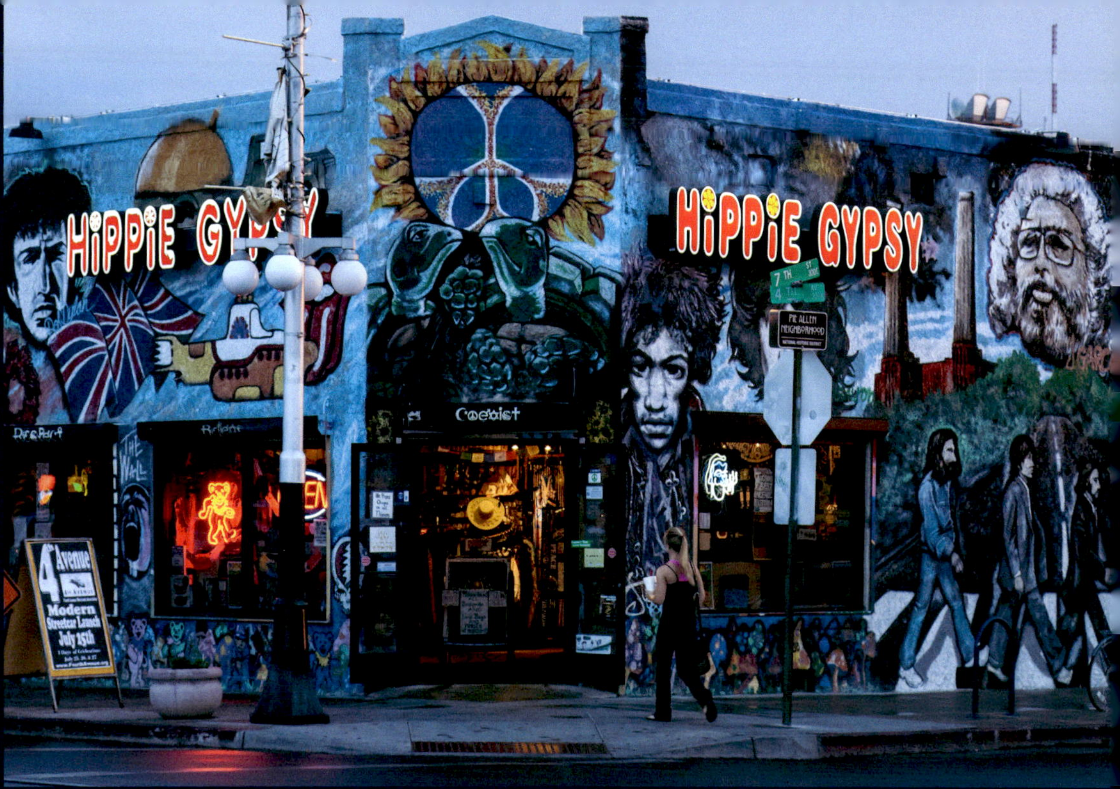

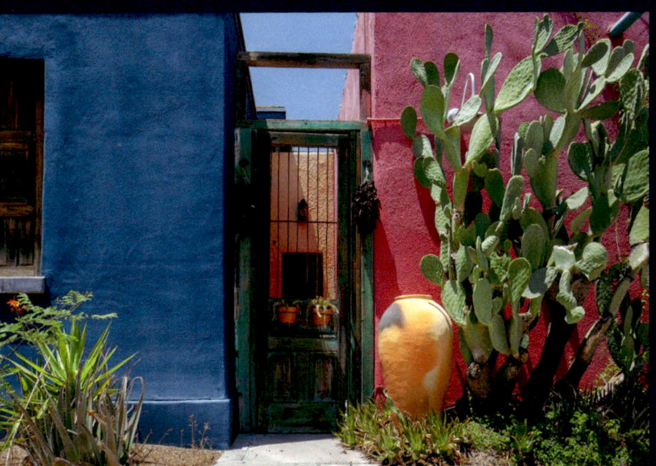

Above, right: A corner building serves as a canvas in Tucson's artsy Historic Fourth Avenue District. LARRY LINDAHL

Above, left: At Tucson's historic Hotel Congress, you can dine, imbibe, enjoy live music, and sleep it all off in a building famous for its role in the capture of gangster John Dillinger in 1934. LARRY LINDAHL

Left: Brightly painted adobe houses give Tucson's Barrio Historico the feel of a traditional Mexican village. LARRY LINDAHL

Facing page: Tucson's Cathedral of St. Augustine was founded as a chapel in 1776, with completion of the cathedral in 1868. A century later, the cathedral underwent restoration to preserve its Mexican baroque façade. LARRY LINDAHL

Right: A painted lady butterfly rests gracefully on a bouquet of western sneezeweed. JAKE CASE

Far right: Brittlebush blooms on the cactus-clad slopes above Bartlett Lake as the last rays of sun kiss Maverick Mountain. JAKE CASE

Below: Aravaipa Creek, a rare continuously-flowing spring-fed stream in the Sonoran Desert, catches a glimmer of golden light on an early spring evening. JAKE CASE

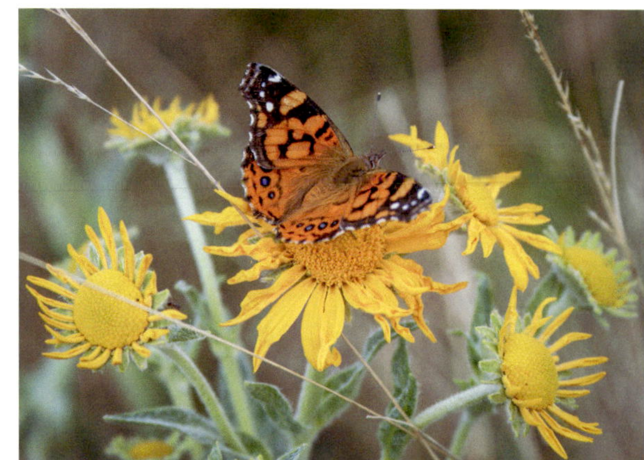

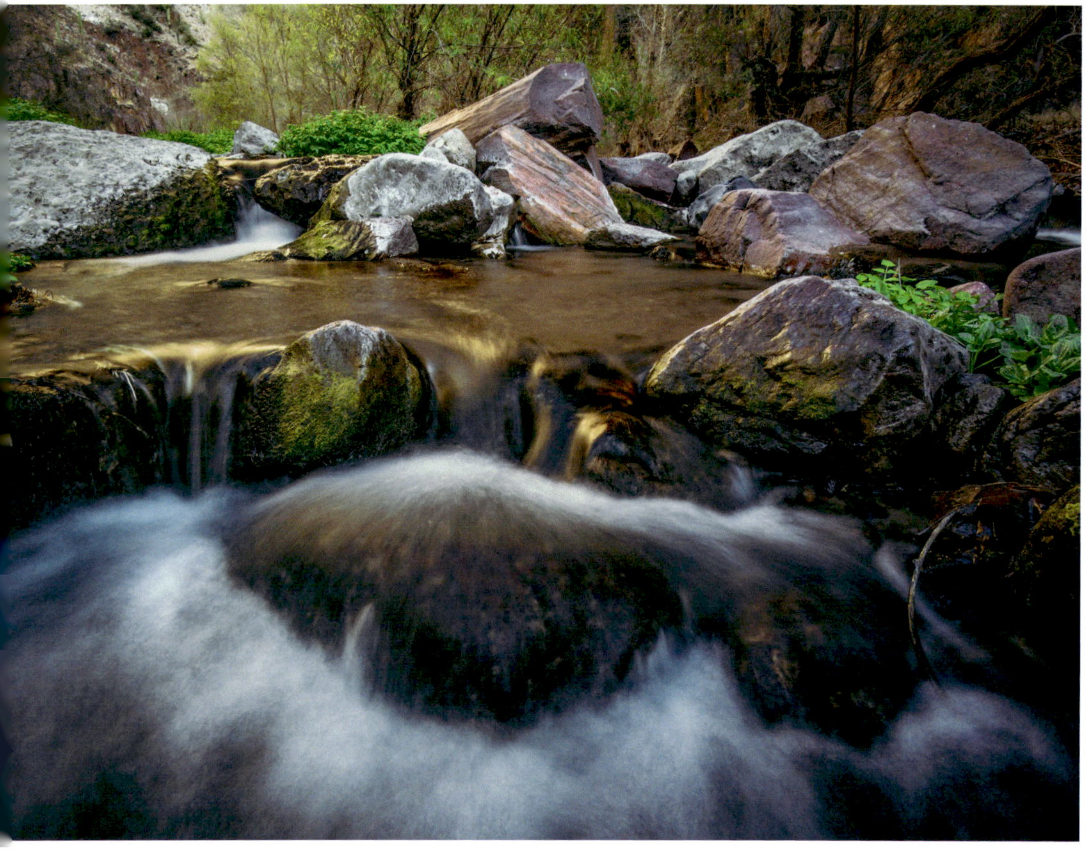

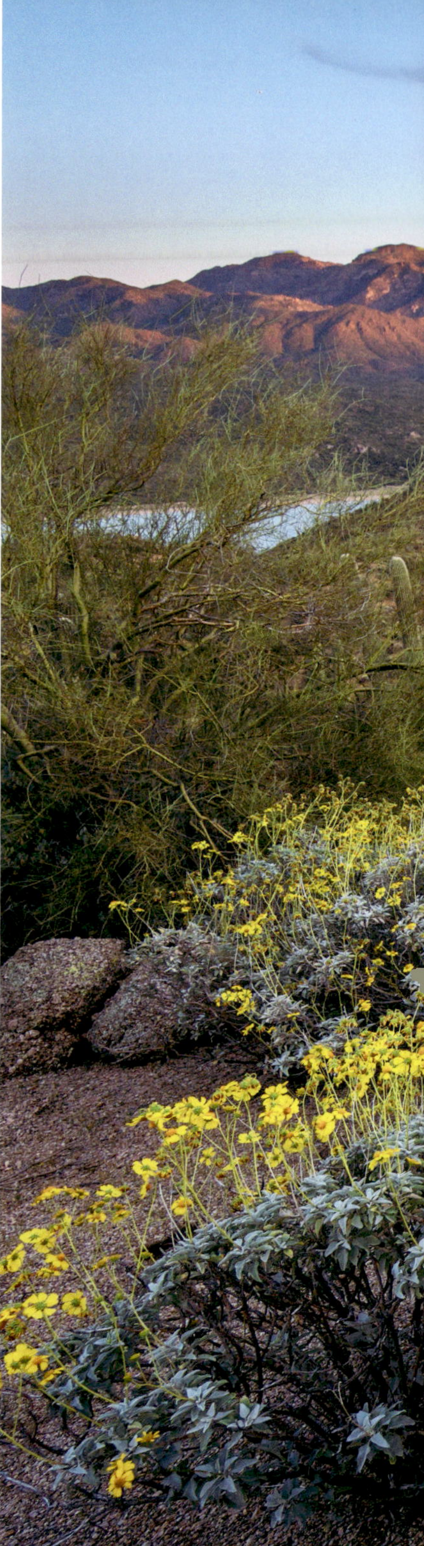

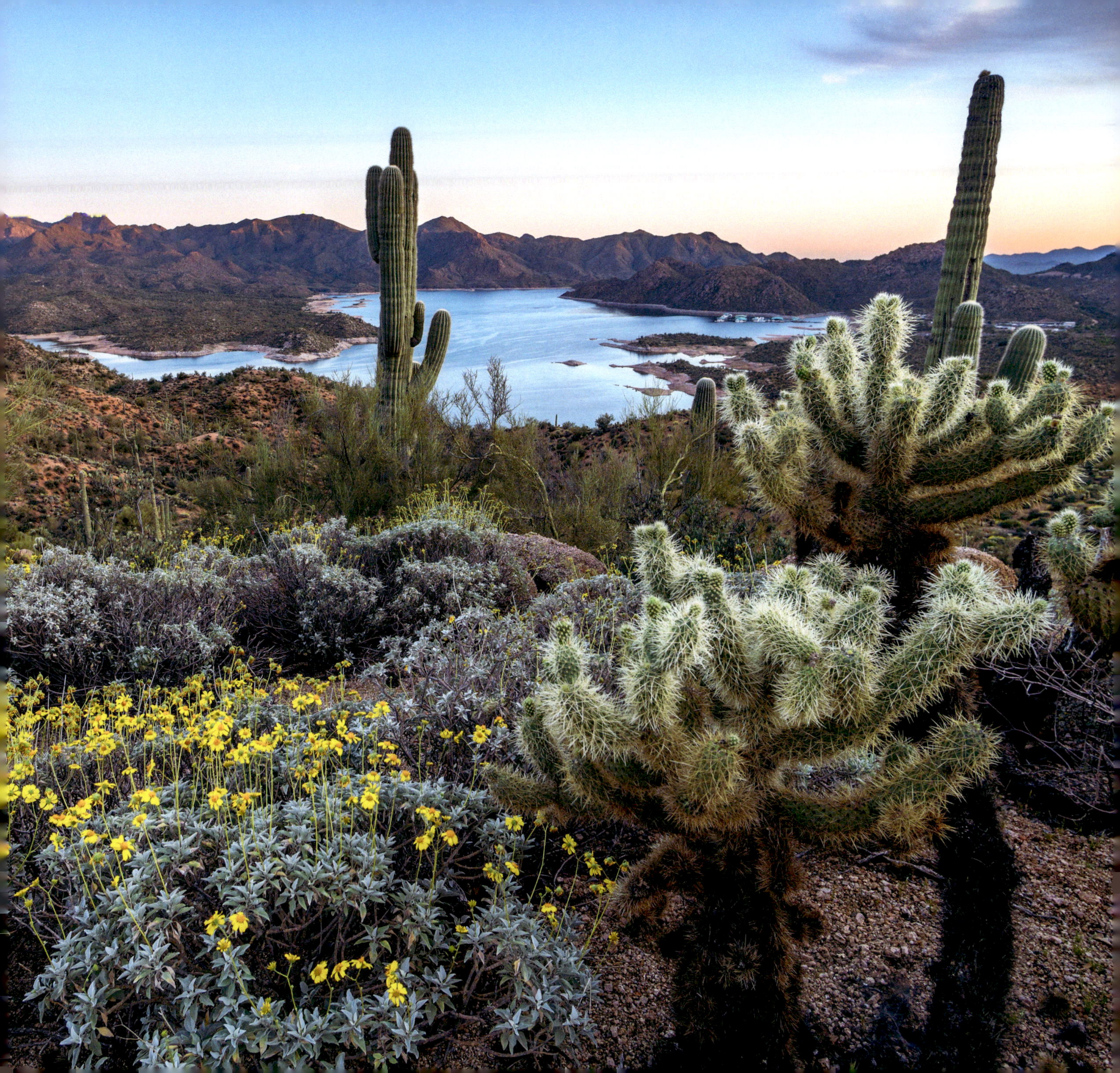

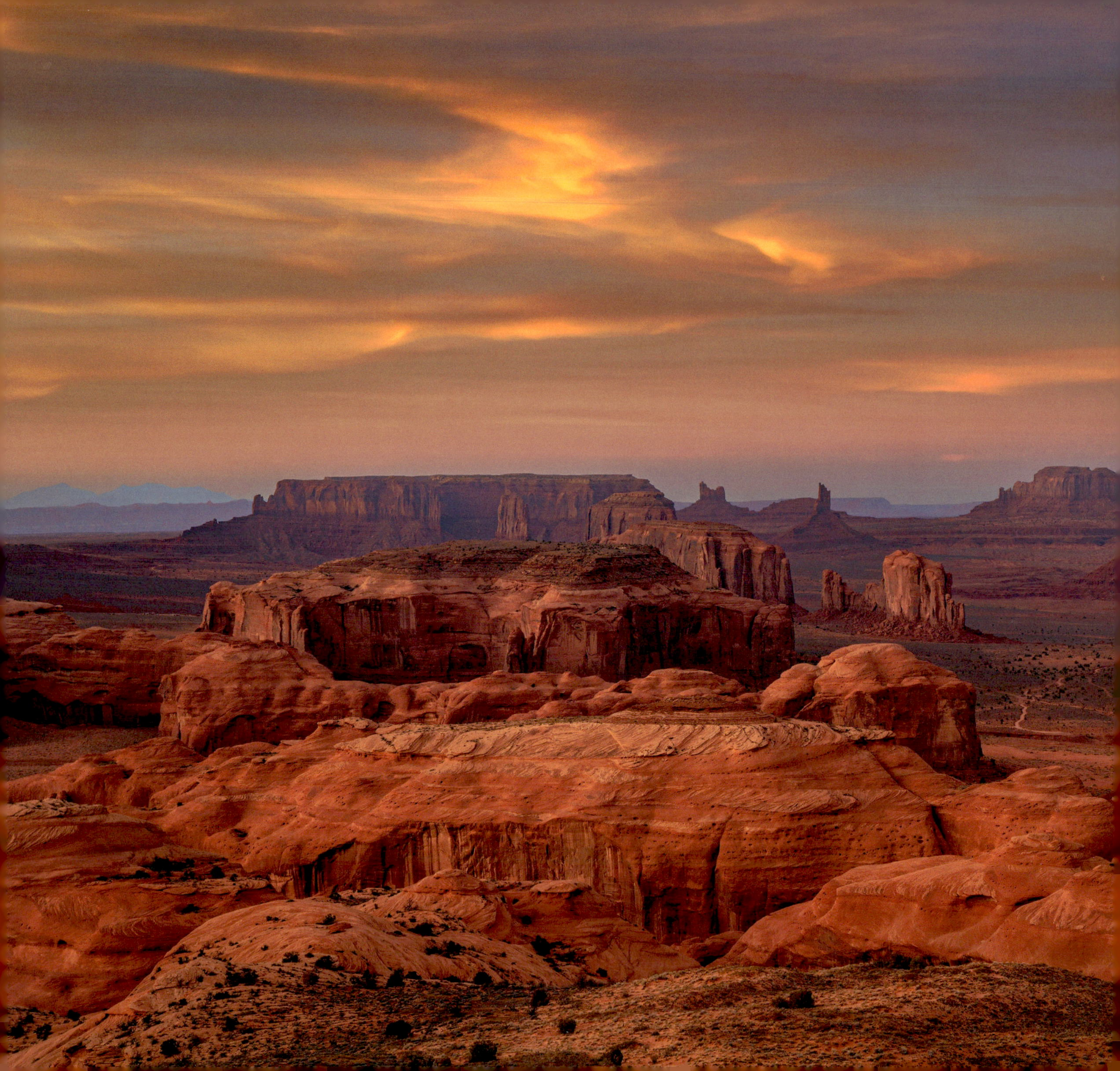

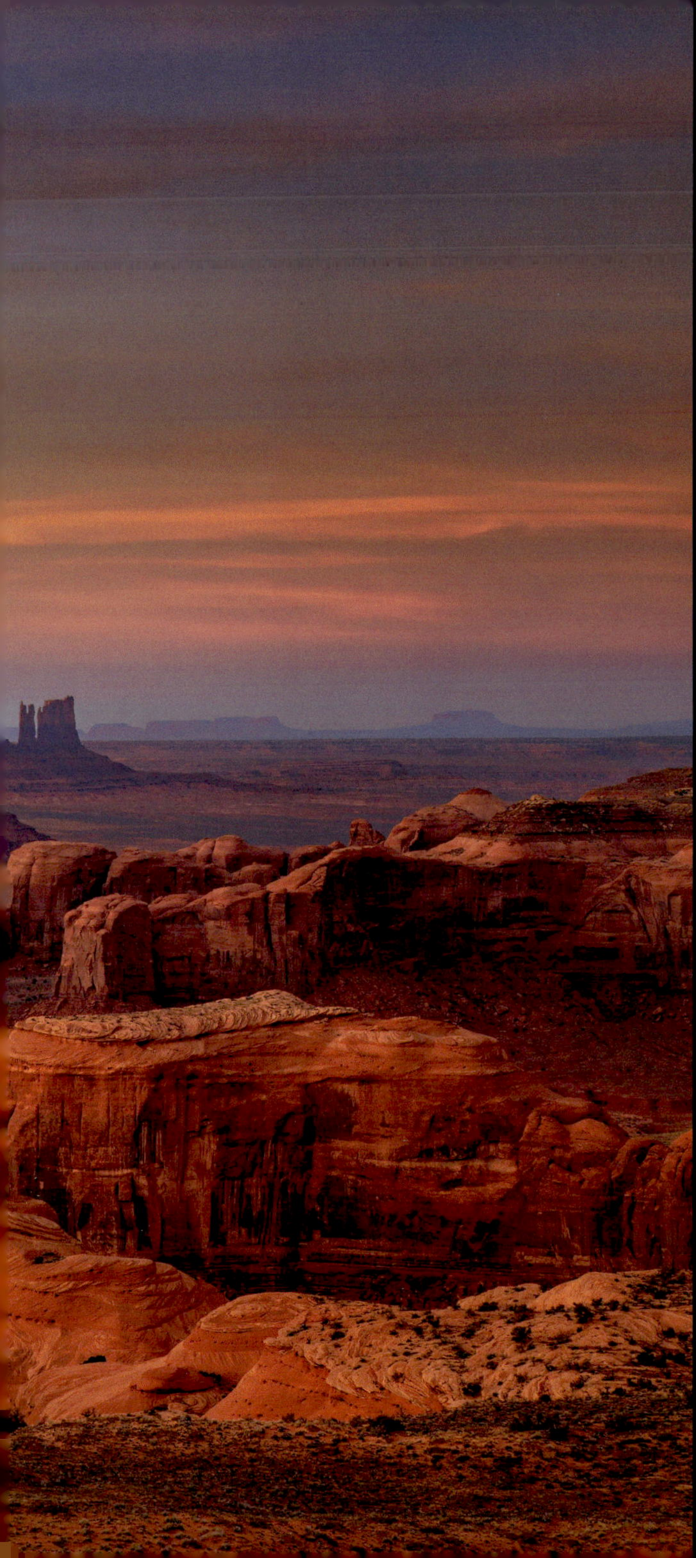

Left: Navajo guides enable visitor access to Hunts Mesa and this stunning vista of Monument Valley where many Western movies were once filmed. LARRY LINDAHL

Below: A trio of saguaros form dramatic silhouettes during a fiery December sunset near Lake Pleasant. Their mature arms indicate the cacti are well over 100 years old. JAKE CASE

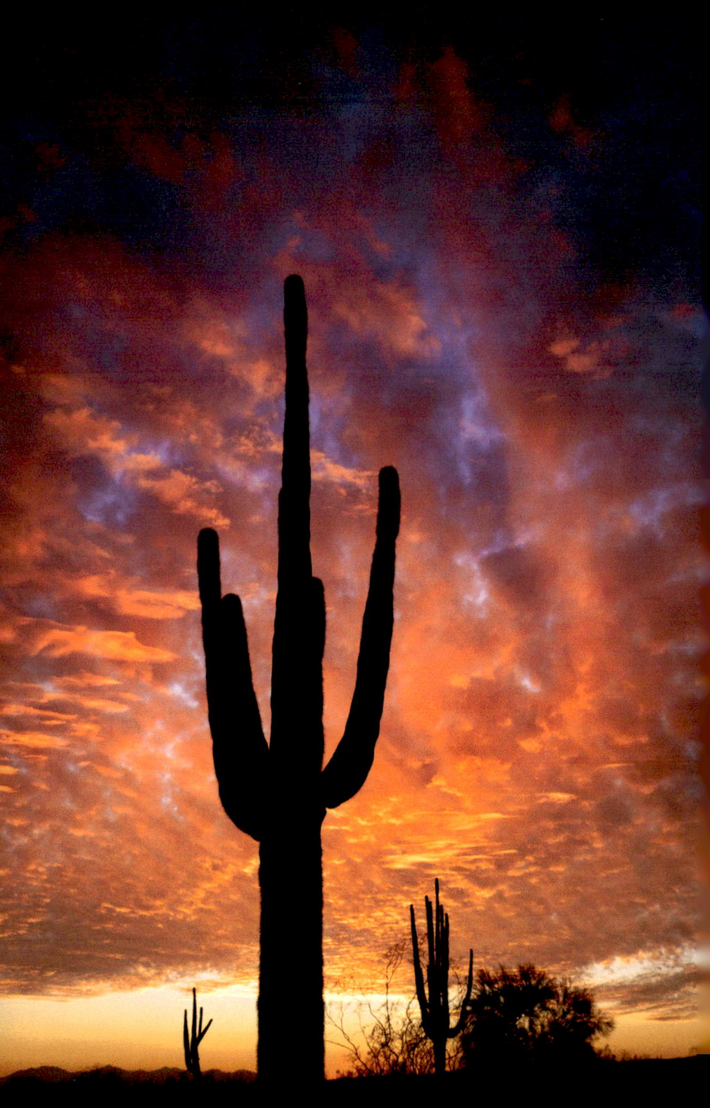

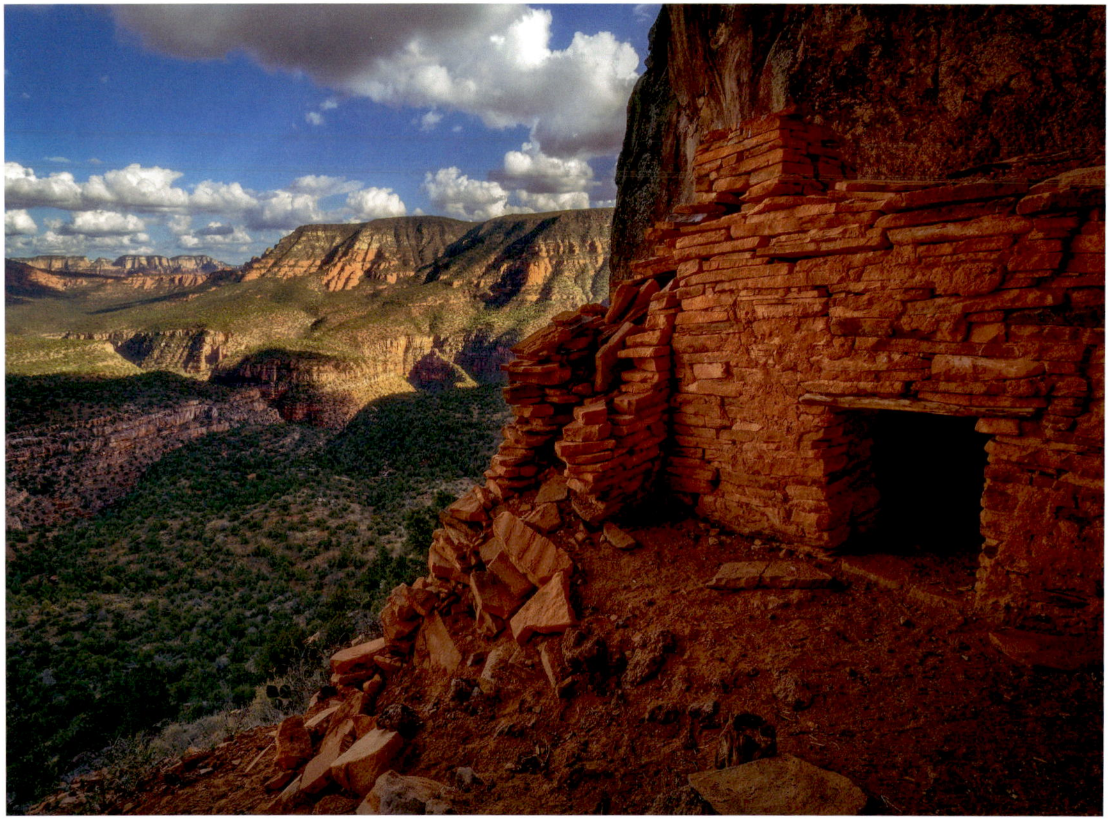

Above: An ancient cliff dwelling of the Sinagua culture overlooks Sycamore Canyon Wilderness Area. LARRY LINDAHL

Right: The "late-bloomer" of the Sonoran Desert, a giant saguaro shows its creamy white flowers on a May afternoon in the Superstition Wilderness. JAKE CASE

Far right: Oak Creek slithers over sandstone at Slide Rock State Park north of Sedona. LARRY LINDAHL

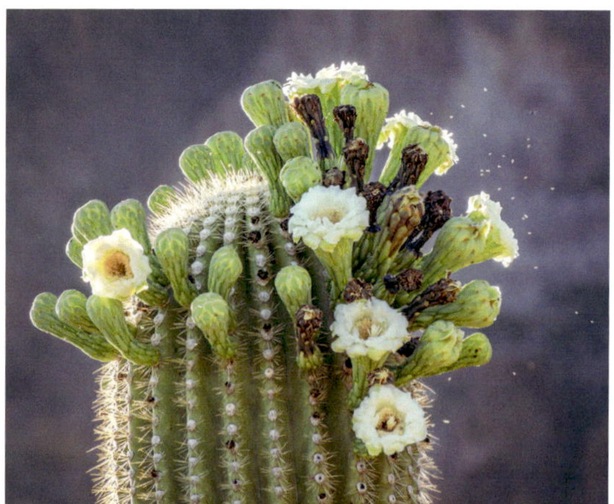

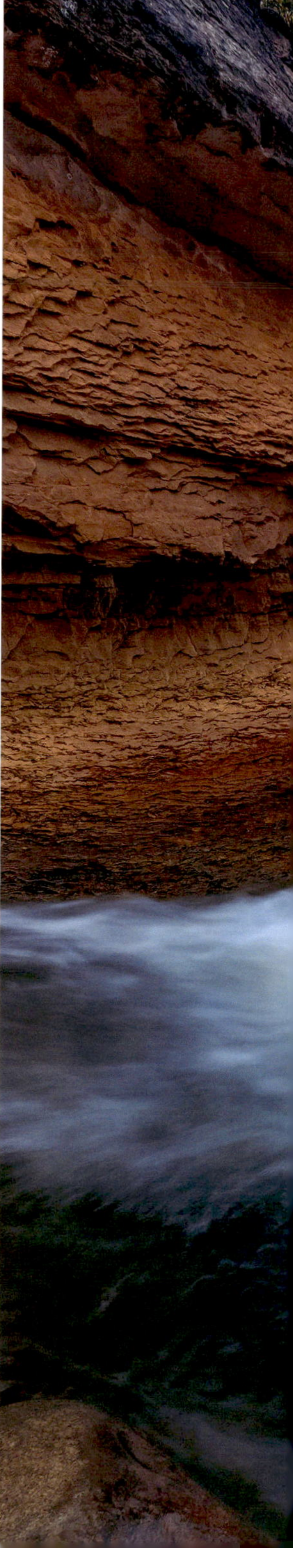

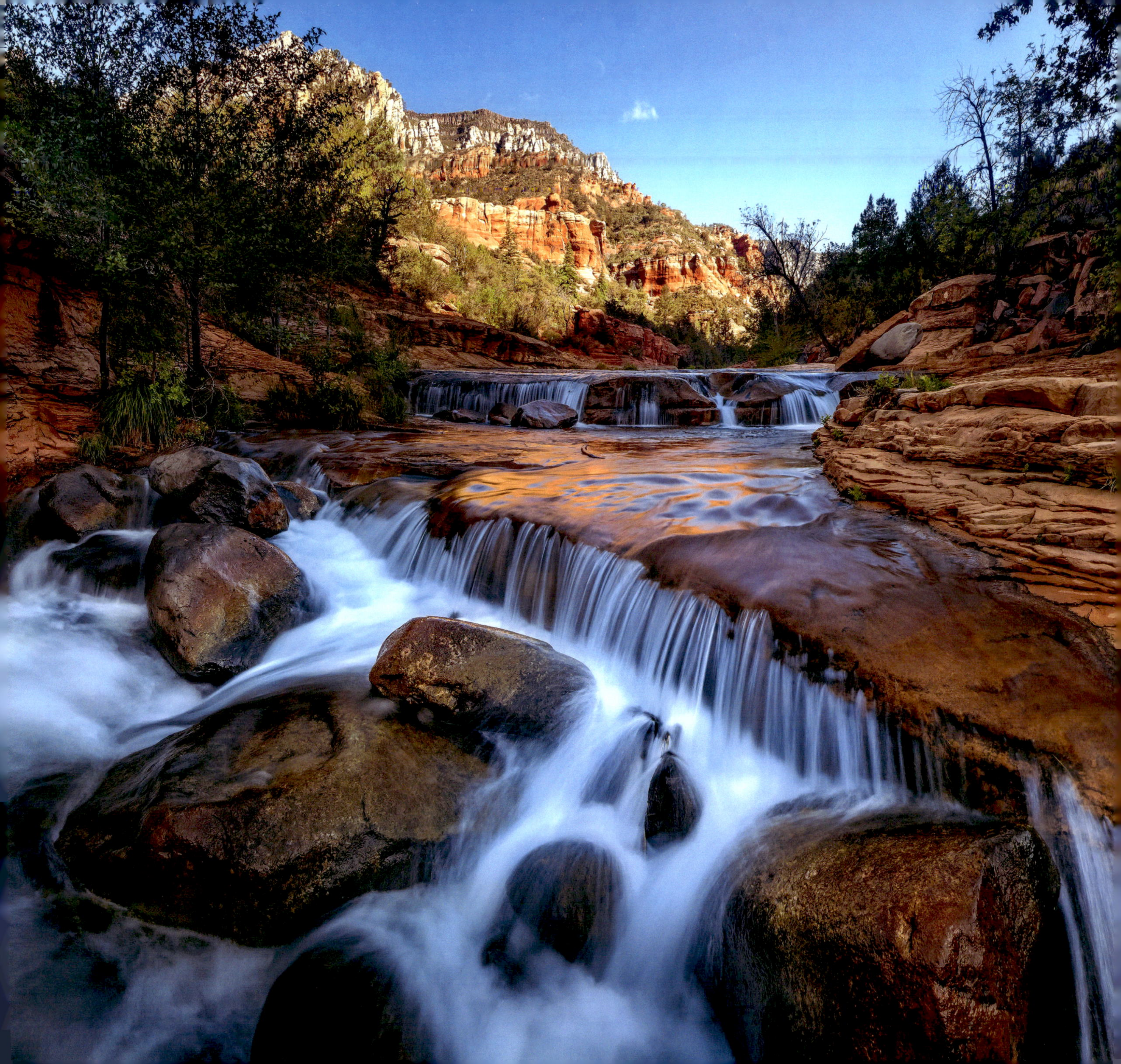

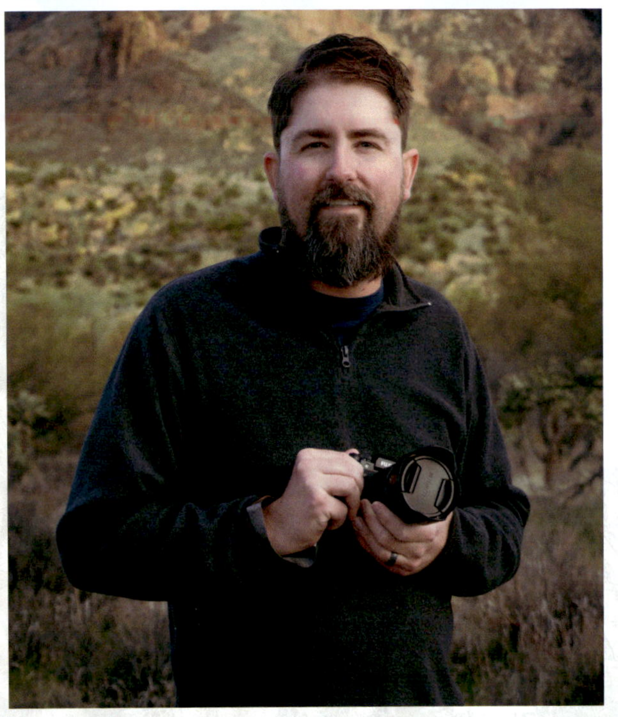

A second-generation Arizonan, **JAKE CASE** is a naturalist, photographer, and writer based in Phoenix. An alumnus of Northern Arizona University and a geographer by education, he has worked as a tour guide at the Grand Canyon South Rim, a park ranger at Glen Canyon National Recreation Area, and a docent at Taliesin West. As an avid hiker and backpacker, Jake is passionate about the natural areas of the Southwest, and sharing those wonders with the world. Jake's mission is to inspire others to see the value in nature. He spends much of his time exploring and photographing Arizona and beyond with his wife and daughter. To see more of his work, visit www.jakecase.com

LARRY LINDAHL seeks to inspire with vibrant, engaging, and thoughtful travel and landscape photography. As a professional for over thirty years, he has collected a diverse portfolio from road trips across Route 66 to river trips through Grand Canyon. His images are featured in multiple photography books including *Grand Canyon: A Photographic Journey*, *Secret Sedona*, and *The Ancient Southwest*. He is published in magazines such as *Arizona Highways, Southwest Art, Backpacker,* and *Condé Nast Traveler*. His work is also on display in corporate collections, national parks, and the Smithsonian Institute. Larry resides in Sedona, Arizona, his home for over thirty years. To learn more about his photography, visit LarryLindahl.com

Background photo: Wildflowers and cacti in the Phoenix Sonoran Preserve on a spring morning. JAKE CASE